Constitution

of the

Commonwealth of Pennsylvania

CONSTITUTION OF THE COMMONWEALTH OF PENNSYLVANIA

WE, the people of the Commonwealth of Pennsylvania, grateful to Almighty God for the blessings of civil and religious liberty, and humbly invoking His guidance, do ordain and establish this Constitution.

Article I

DECLARATION OF RIGHTS

That the general, great and essential principles of liberty and free government may be recognized and unalterably established, WE DECLARE THAT -

Inherent Rights of Mankind
Section 1.

All men are born equally free and independent, and have certain inherent and indefeasible rights, among which are those of enjoying and defending life and liberty, of acquiring, possessing and protecting property and reputation, and of pursuing their own happiness.

Political Powers
Section 2.

All power is inherent in the people, and all free governments are founded on their authority and instituted for their peace, safety and happiness. For the advancement of these ends they have at all times an inalienable and indefeasible right to alter, reform or abolish their government in such manner as they may think proper.

Religious Freedom

Section 3.

All men have a natural and indefeasible right to worship Almighty God according to the dictates of their own consciences; no man can of right be compelled to attend, erect or support any place of worship or to maintain any ministry against his consent; no human authority can, in any case whatever, control or interfere with the rights of conscience, and no preference shall ever be given by law to any religious establishments or modes of worship.

Religion
Section 4.

No person who acknowledges the being of a God and a future state of rewards and punishments shall, on account of his religious sentiments, be disqualified to hold any office or place of trust or profit under this Commonwealth.

Elections
Section 5.

Elections shall be free and equal; and no power, civil or military, shall at any time interfere to prevent the free exercise of the right of suffrage.

Trial by Jury
Section 6.

Trial by jury shall be as heretofore, and the right thereof remain inviolate. The General assembly may provide, however, by law, that a verdict may be rendered by not less than five-sixths of the jury in any civil case. Furthermore, in criminal cases, the Commonwealth shall have the same right to trial by jury as does the accused.

Freedom of Press and Speech; Libels
Section 7.

The printing press shall be free to every person who may undertake to examine the proceedings of the Legislature or any branch of government, and no law shall ever by made to restrain the right thereof. The free communication of thoughts and opinions is one of the invaluable rights of man, and every citizen may freely speak, write and print on any subject, being responsible for the abuse of that liberty. No conviction shall be had in any prosecution for the publication of papers relating to the official conduct of officers or men in public capacity, or to any other matter proper for public investigation or information, where the fact that such publication was not maliciously or negligently made shall be established to the satisfaction of the jury; and in all indictments for libels the jury shall have the right to determine the law and the facts, under the direction of the court, as in other cases.

Security From Searches and Seizures
Section 8.

The people shall be secure in their persons, houses, papers and possessions from unreasonable searches and seizures, and no warrant to search any place or to seize any person or things shall issue without describing them as nearly as may be, nor without probable cause, supported by oath or affirmation subscribed by the affiant.

Rights of Accused in Criminal Prosecutions
Section 9.

In all criminal prosecutions the accused hath a right to be heard by himself and his counsel, to demand the nature and cause of the accusation against him, to be confronted with the witnesses against him, to have compulsory process for obtaining witnesses in his favor, and in prosecutions by indictment or information, a speedy public trial by an impartial jury of the vicinage; he cannot be compelled to give evidence against himself, nor can he be deprived of his life, liberty or property, unless by the judgment of his peers or the law of the land. The use of a suppressed voluntary admission or voluntary confession to impeach the credibility of a person may be permitted and shall not be construed as compelling a person to give evidence against himself.

Initiation of Criminal Proceedings; Twice in
Jeopardy; Eminent Domain
Section 10.

Except as hereinafter provided no person shall, for any indictable offense, be proceeded against criminally by information, except in cases arising in the land or naval forces, or in the militia, when in actual service, in time of war or public danger, or by leave of the court for oppression or misdemeanor in office. Each of the several courts of common pleas may, with the approval of the Supreme Court, provide for the initiation of criminal proceedings therein by information filed in the manner provided by law. No person shall, for the same offense, be twice put in jeopardy of life or limb; nor shall private property be taken or applied to public use, without authority of law and without just compensation being first made or secured.

Courts to Be Open; Suits Against the
Commonwealth
Section 11.

All courts shall be open; and every man for an injury done him in his lands, goods, person or reputation shall have remedy by due course of law, and eight and justice administered without sale, denial or delay. Suits may be brought against the Commonwealth in such manner, in such courts and in such cases as the Legislature may by law direct.

Power of Suspending Laws
Section 12.

No power of suspending laws shall be exercised unless by the Legislature or by its authority.

Bail, Fines and Punishments
Section 13.

Excessive bail shall not be required, nor excessive fines imposed, nor cruel punishments inflicted.

Prisoners to be Bailable; Habeas Corpus
Section 14.

All prisoners shall be bailable by sufficient sureties, unless for capital offenses or for offenses for which the maximum sentence is life imprisonment or unless no condition or combination of conditions other than imprisonment will reasonably assure the safety of any person and the community when the proof is evident or presumption great; and the privilege of the writ of habeas corpus shall not be suspended, unless when in case of rebellion or invasion the public safety may require it.

Special Criminal Tribunals
Section 15.

No commission shall issue creating special temporary criminal tribunals to try particular individuals or particular classes of cases.

Insolvent Debtors
Section 16.

The person of a debtor, where there is not strong presumption of fraud, shall not be continued in prison after delivering up his estate for the benefit of his creditors in such manner as shall be prescribed by law.

Ex Post Facto Laws; Impairment of Contracts
Section 17.

No ex post facto law, nor any law impairing the obligation of contracts, or making irrevocable any grant of special privileges or immunities, shall be passed.

Attainder
Section 18.

No person shall be attained of treason or felony by the Legislature.

Attainder Limited
Section 19.

No attainder shall work corruption of blood, nor, except during the life of the offender, forfeiture of estate to the Commonwealth.

Right of Petition
Section 20.

The citizens have a right in a peaceable manner to assemble together for their common good, and to apply to those invested with the powers of government for redress of grievances or other proper purposes by petition, address or remonstrance.

Right to Bear Arms
Section 21.

The right of the citizens to bear arms in defense of themselves and the State shall not be questioned.

Standing Army; Military Subordinate to Civil Power
Section 22.

No standing army shall, in time of peace, be kept up without the consent of the Legislature, and the military shall in all cases and at all times be in strict subordination to the civil power.

Quartering of Troops
Section 23.

No soldier shall in time of peace be quartered in any house without the consent of the owner, nor in time of war but in a manner to be prescribed by law.

Titles and Offices
Section 24.

The Legislature shall not grant any title of nobility of hereditary distinction, nor create any office the appointment to which shall be for a longer term than during good behavior.

Reservation of Powers in People
Section 25.

To guard against the transgressions of the high powers which we have delegated, we declare that everything in this article is excepted out of the general powers of government and shall forever remain inviolate.

No Discrimination by Commonwealth and Its Political Subdivisions
Section 26.

Neither the Commonwealth nor any political subdivision thereof shall deny to any person the enjoyment of any civil right, nor discriminate against any person in the exercise of any civil right.

Natural Resources and the Public Estate
Section 27.

The people have a right to clean air, pure water, and to the preservation of the natural, scenic, historic and esthetic values of the environment. Pennsylvania's public natural resources are the common property of all the people, including generations yet to come. As trustee of these resources, the Commonwealth shall conserve and maintain them for the benefit of all the people.

Prohibition Against Denial or Abridgment of Equality of Rights Because of Sex
Section 28.

Equality of rights under the law shall not be denied or abridged in the Commonwealth of Pennsylvania because of the sex of the individual.

Article II

THE LEGISLATURE

Legislative Power
Section 1.

The legislative power of this Commonwealth shall be vested in a General Assembly, which shall consist of a Senate and a House of Representatives.

Election of Members; Vacancies
Section 2.

Members of the General Assembly shall be chosen at the general election every second year. Their term of service shall begin on the first day of December next after their election. Whenever a vacancy shall occur in either House, the presiding officer thereof shall issue a writ of election to fill such vacancy for the remainder of the term.

Terms of Members
Section 3.

Senators shall be elected for the term of four years and Representatives for the term of two years.

Sessions
Section 4.

The General Assembly shall be a continuing body during the term for which its Representatives are elected. It shall meet at twelve o'clock noon on the first Tuesday of January each year. Special sessions shall be called by the Governor on petition of a majority of the members elected to each House or may be called by the Governor whenever in his opinion the public interest requires.

Qualifications of Members
Section 5.

Senators shall be at least twenty-five years of age and Representatives twenty-one years of age. They shall have been citizens and inhabitants of the State four years, and inhabitants of their respective districts one year next before their election (unless absent on the public business of the United States or of this State) and shall reside in their respective districts during their terms of service.

Disqualification to Hold Other Office
Section 6.

No Senator or Representative shall, during the time for which he was elected, be appointed to any civil office under this Commonwealth to which a salary, fee of perquisite is attached. No member of Congress or other person holding any office (except of attorney-at law or in the national guard or in a reserve component of the armed forces of the United States) under the United States of this Commonwealth to which a salary, fee or perquisite is attached shall be a member of either House during his continuance in office.

Ineligibility by Criminal Convictions
Section 7.

No person hereafter convicted of embezzlement of public moneys, bribery, perjury or other infamous crime, shall be eligible to the General Assembly, or capable of holding any office of trust or profit in this Commonwealth.

Compensation
Section 8.

The members of the General Assembly shall receive such salary and mileage for regular and special sessions as shall be fixed by law, and no other compensation whatever, whether for service upon committee or otherwise. No member of either House shall during the term for which he may have been elected, receive any increase of salary, or mileage, under any law passed during such term.

Election of Officers; Judge of Election and Qualifications of Members
Section 9.

The Senate shall, at the beginning and close of each regular session and at such other times as may be necessary, elect one of its members President protempore, who shall perform the duties of the Lieutenant Governor shall be vacant. The House of Representatives shall elect one of its members as Speaker. Each House shall choose its other officers, and shall judge of the election and qualifications of its members.

Quorum

Section 10.

A majority of each House shall constitute a quorum, but a smaller number may adjourn from day to day and compel the attendance of absent members.

Powers of Each House; Expulsion
Section 11.

Each House shall have power to determine the rules of its proceedings and punish its members or other persons for contempt or disorderly behavior in its presence, to enforce obedience to its process, to protect its members against violence or offers of bribes or private solicitation, and, with the concurrence of two-thirds, to expel a member, but not a second time for the same cause, and shall have all other powers necessary for the Legislature of a free State. A member expelled for corruption shall not thereafter be eligible to either House, and punishment for contempt or disorderly behavior shall not bar an indictment for the same offense.

Journals; Yeas and Nays
Section 12.

Each House shall keep a journal of its proceedings and from time to time publish the same, except such parts as require secrecy, and the yeas and nays of the members on any question shall, at the desire of any two of them, be entered on the journal.

Open Sessions
Section 13.

The sessions of each House and of committees of the whole shall be open, unless when the business is such as ought to be kept secret.

Adjournments
Section 14.

Neither House shall, without the consent of the other, adjourn for more than three days, nor to any other place than that in which the two Houses shall be sitting.

Privileges of Members

Section 15.

The members of the General Assembly shall in all cases, except treason, felony, violation of their oath of office, and breach of surety of the peace, be privileged from arrest during their attendance at the sessions of their respective Houses and in going to and returning from the same; and for any speech or debate in either House they shall not be questioned in any other place.

Legislative Districts
Section 16.

The Commonwealth shall be divided into fifty senatorial and two hundred three representative districts, which shall be composed of compact and contiguous territory as nearly equal in population as practicable. Each senatorial district shall elect one Senator, and each representative district one Representative. Unless absolutely necessary no county, city, incorporated town, borough, township or ward shall be divided in forming either a senatorial or representative district.

Legislative Reapportionment Commission
Section 17.

(a) In each year following the year of the Federal decennial census, a Legislative Reapportionment Commission shall be constituted for the purpose of reapportioning the Commonwealth. The commission shall act by a majority of its entire membership.

(b) The commission shall consist of five members: four of whom shall be the majority and minority leaders of both the Senate and the House of Representatives, or deputies appointed by each of them, and a chairman selected as hereinafter provided. No later than 60 days following the official reporting of the Federal decennial census as required by Federal law, the four members shall be certified by the President Pro Tempore of the Senate and the Speaker of the House of Representatives to the elections officer of the Commonwealth who under law shall have supervision over elections. The four members within 45 days after their certification shall select the fifth member, who shall serve as chairman of the commission, and shall immediately certify his name to such elections officer. The chairman shall be a citizen of the Commonwealth other than a local, State or Federal official; holding an office to which compensation is attached. If the four members fail to select the fifth member within the time prescribed, a majority of the entire membership of the Supreme Court within thirty days thereafter shall appoint the chairman as aforesaid and certify his appointment to such elections officer. Any vacancy in the commission shall be filled within fifteen days in the same manner in which such position was originally filled.

(c) No later than ninety days after either the commission has been duly certified or the population data for the Commonwealth as determined by the Federal decennial census are available, whichever is later in time, the commission shall file a preliminary reapportionment plan with such elections officer. The commission shall have thirty days after filling the preliminary plan to make corrections in the plan. Any person aggrieved by the preliminary plan shall have the same thirty-day period to file exceptions with the commission in which case the commission shall thirty days after the date the exceptions were filled to prepare and file with such elections officer a revised reapportionment plan. If no exceptions are filled within thirty days, or if filed and acted upon, the commission's plan shall be final and have the force of law.

(d) Any aggrieved person may file an appeal from the final plan directly to the Supreme Court within thirty days after the filing thereof. If the appellant establishes that the final plan is contrary to law, the Supreme Court shall issue an order remanding the plan to the commission and directing the commission to reapportion the Commonwealth in a manner not inconsistent with such order.

(e) When the Supreme Court has finally decided an appeal or when the last day for filing an appeal has passed with no appeal taken, the reapportionment plan shall have the force of law and the districts therein provided shall be used thereafter in elections to the General Assembly until the next reapportionment as required under this section 17.

(f) Any district which does not include the residence from which a member of the Senate was elected whether or not scheduled for election at the next general election shall elect a Senator at such election.

(g) The General Assembly shall appropriate sufficient funds for the compensation and expenses of members and staff appointed by the commission, and other necessary expenses. The members of the commission shall be entitled to such compensation for their services as the General Assembly from time to time shall determine but no part thereof shall be paid until a preliminary plan is filed. If a preliminary plan is filed but the commission fails to file a revised or final plan within the time prescribed, the commission members shall forfeit all right to compensation not paid.

(h) If a preliminary, revised or final reapportionment plan is not filed by the commission within the time prescribed by this section, unless the time be extended by the Supreme Court for cause shown, the Supreme Court shall immediately proceed on its own motion to reapportion the Commonwealth.

(i) Any reapportionment plan filed by the commission, or ordered or prepared by the Supreme Court upon the failure of the commission to act, shall be published by the elections officer once in at least one newspaper of general circulation in each senatorial and representative district. The publication shall contain a map of the Commonwealth showing the complete reapportionment of the General Assembly by districts, and a map showing the reapportionment districts in the area normally served by the newspaper in which the publication is male. The publication shall also state the population of the senatorial and representative districts having the smallest and largest population and the percentage variation of such districts from the average population for senatorial and representative districts.

Article III

LEGISLATION

A. Procedure

Passage of Laws
Section 1.

No law shall be passed except by bill, and no bill shall be so altered or amended, on its passage through either House, as to change its original purpose.

Reference to Committee; Printing
Section 2.

No bill shall be considered unless referred to a committee, printed for the use of the members and returned therefrom.

Form of Bills
Section 3.

No bill shall be passed containing more than one subject, which shall be clearly expressed in its title, except a general appropriation bill or a bill codifying or compiling the law or a part thereof.

Consideration of Bills
Section 4.

Every bill shall be considered on three different days in each House. All amendments made thereto shall be printed for the use of the members before the final vote is taken on the bill and before the final vote is taken, upon written request addressed to the presiding officer of either House by at least twenty-five percent of the members elected to that House, any bill shall be read at length in that House. No bill shall become a law, unless on its final passage the vote is taken by yeas and nays, the names of the persons voting for and against it are entered on the journal, and a majority of the members elected to each House is recorded thereon as voting in its favor.

Concurring in Amendments; Conference
Committee Reports
Section 5.

No amendment to bills by one House shall be concurred in by the other, except by the vote of a majority of the members elected thereto, taken by yeas and nays, and the names of those voting recorded upon the journals.

Revival and Amendment of Laws
Section 6.

No law shall be revived, amended, or the provisions thereof extended or conferred, by reference to its title only, but so much thereof as is revived, amended, extended or conferred shall be re-enacted and published at length.

Notice of Local and Special Bills
Section 7.

No local or special bill shall be passed unless notice of the intention to apply therefor shall have been published in the locality where the matter or the thing to be effected may be situated, which notice shall be at least thirty days prior to the introduction into the General Assembly of such bill and in the manner to be provided by law; the evidence of such notice having been published, shall be exhibited in the General Assembly, before such act shall be passed.

Signing of Bills
Section 8.

The presiding officer of each House shall, in the presence of the House over which he presides, sign all bills and joint resolutions passed by the General Assembly, after their titles have been publicly read immediately before signing; and the fact of signing shall be entered on the journal.

Action on Concurrent Orders and Resolutions

Section 9.

Every order, resolution or vote, to which the concurrence of both Houses may be necessary, except on the question of adjournment, shall be presented to the Governor and before it shall take effect be approved by him, or being disapproved, shall be repassed by two-thirds of both Houses according to the rules and limitations prescribed in case of a bill.

Revenue Bills
Section 10.

All bills for raising revenue shall originate in the House of Representatives, but the Senate may propose amendments as in other bills.

Appropriation Bills
Section 11.

The general appropriation bill shall embrace nothing but appropriations for the executive, legislative and judicial departments of the Commonwealth, for the public debt and for public schools. All other appropriations shall be made by separate bills, each embracing but one subject.

Legislation Designated by Governor at Special Sessions
Section 12.

When the General Assembly shall be convened in special session, there shall be no legislation upon subjects other than those designated in the proclamation of the Governor calling such session.

Vote Denied Members with Personal Interest
Section 12.

A member who has a personal or private interest in any measure or bill proposed or pending before the General Assembly shall disclose the fact to the House of which he is a member, and shall not vote thereon. B. Education

Public School System
Section 14.

The General Assembly shall provide for the maintenance and support of a thorough and efficient system of public education to serve the needs of the Commonwealth.

Public School Money Not Available to Sectarian Schools
Section 15.

No money raised for the support of the public schools of the Commonwealth shall be appropriated to or used for the support of any sectarian school. C. National Guard

National Guard to be Organized and Maintained
Section 16.

The citizens of this Commonwealth shall be armed, organized and disciplined for its defense when and in such manner as may be directed by law. The General Assembly shall provide for maintaining the National Guard by appropriations from the Treasury of the Commonwealth, and may exempt from State military service persons having conscientious scruples against bearing arms. D. Other Legislation Specifically Authorized

Appointment of Legislative Officers and
Employees
Section 17.

The General Assembly shall prescribe by law the number, duties and compensation of the officers and employees of each House, and no payment shall be made from the State Treasury, or be in any way authorized, to any person, except to an acting officer or employee elected or appointed in pursuance of law.

Compensation Laws Allowed to General Assembly
Section 18.

The General Assembly may enact laws requiring the payment by employers, or employers and employees jointly, of reasonable compensation for injuries to employees arising in the course of their employment, and for occupational diseases of employees, whether or not such injuries or diseases result in death, and regardless of fault of employer or employee, and fixing the basis of ascertainment of such compensation and the maximum and minimum limits thereof, and providing special or general remedies for the collection thereof; but in no other cases shall the General Assembly limit the amount to be recovered for injuries resulting in death, or for injuries to persons or property, and in case of death from such injuries, the right of action shall survive, and the General Assembly shall prescribe for whose benefit such actions shall be prosecuted. No act shall prescribe any limitations of time within which suits may be brought against corporations for injuries to persons or property, or for other causes different from those fixed by general laws regulating actions against natural persons, and such acts now existing are avoided.

Appropriations for Support of Widows and
Orphans of Persons Who Served in the Armed
Forces
Section 19.

The General Assembly may make appropriations of money to institutions wherein the widows of persons who served in the armed forces are supported or assisted, or the orphans of persons who served in the armed forces are maintained and educated; but such appropriations shall be applied exclusively to the support of such widows and orphans.

Classification of Municipalities
Section 20.

The Legislature shall have power to classify counties, cities, boroughs, school districts, and townships according to population, and all laws passed relating to each class, and all laws passed relating to, and regulating procedure and proceedings in court with reference to, any class, shall be deemed general legislation within the meaning of this Constitution.

Land Title Registration
Section 21.

Laws may be passed providing for a system of registering, transferring, insuring of and guaranteeing land titles by the State, or by the counties thereof, and for settling and determining adverse or other claims to and interest in lands the titles to which are so registered, transferred, insured, and guaranteed; and for the creation and collection of indemnity funds; and for carrying the system and powers hereby provided for into effect by such existing courts as may be designated by the Legislature. Such laws may provide for continuing the registering, transferring, insuring, and guaranteeing such titles after the first or original registration has been perfected by the court, and provision may be made for raising the necessary funds for expenses and salaries of officers, which shall be paid out of the treasury of the several counties.

State Purchases
Section 22.

The General Assembly shall maintain by law a system of competitive bidding under which all purchases of materials, printing, supplies or other personal property used by the government of this Commonwealth shall so far as practicable be made. The law shall provide that no officer or employee of the Commonwealth shall be in any way interested in any purchase made by the Commonwealth under contract or otherwise.

Change of Venue
Section 23.

The power to change the venue in civil and criminal cases shall be vested in the courts, to be exercised in such manner as shall be provided by law.

Paying Out Public Moneys
Section 24.

No money shall be paid out of the treasury, except on appropriations made by law and on warrant issued by the proper officers; but cash refunds of taxes, licenses, fees and other charges paid or collected, but not legally due, may be paid, as provided by law, without appropriation from the fund into which they were paid on warrant of the proper officer.

Emergency Seats of Government
Section 25.

The General Assembly may provide, by law, during any session, for the continuity of the executive, legislative, and judicial functions of the government of the Commonwealth, and its political subdivisions, and the establishment of emergency seats thereof and any such laws heretofore enacted are validated. Such legislation shall become effective in the event of an attack by an enemy of the United States.

Extra Compensation Prohibited; Claims Against the Commonwealth; Pensions
Section 26.

No bill shall be passed giving any extra compensation to any public officer, servant, employee, agent or contractor after services shall be rendered or contract made, nor providing for the payment of any claim against the Commonwealth without previous authority of law. Provided, however, that nothing in this Constitution shall be construed to prohibit the General Assembly from authorizing the increase of retirement allowances or pensions of members of a retirement or pension system now in effect or hereafter legally constituted by the Commonwealth, its political subdivisions, agencies or instrumentalities, after the termination of the services of said member.

Changes in Term of Office or Salary Prohibited
Section 27.

No law shall extend the term of any public officer, or increase or diminish his salary or emoluments, after his election or appointment. E. Restrictions on Legislative Power

Change of Permanent Location of State Capital
Section 28.

No law changing the permanent location of the Capital of the State shall be valid until the same shall have been submitted to the qualified electors of the Commonwealth at a general election and ratified and approved by them.

Appropriations for Public Assistance, Military Service, Scholarships
Section 29.

No appropriation shall be made for charitable, educational or benevolent purposes to any person or community nor to any denomination and sectarian institution, corporation or association: Provided, that appropriations may be made for pensions of gratuities for military service and to blind persons twenty-one years of age and upwards and for assistance to mothers having dependent children and to aged persons without adequate means of support and in the form of scholarship grants or loans for higher educational purposes to residents of the Commonwealth enrolled in institutions of higher learning except that no scholarship, grants or loans for higher educational purposes shall be given to persons enrolled in a theological seminary or school of theology.

Charitable and Educational Appropriations
Section 30.

No appropriation shall be made to any charitable or educational institution not under the absolute control of the Commonwealth, other than normal schools established by law for the professional training of teachers for the public schools of the State, except by a vote of two-thirds of all the members elected to each House.

Delegation of Certain Powers Prohibited
Section 31.

The General Assembly shall not delegate to any special commission, private corporation or association, any power to make, supervise or interfere with any municipal improvement, money, property or effects, whether held in trust or otherwise, or to levy taxes or perform any municipal function whatever. Notwithstanding the foregoing limitation or any other provision of the Constitution, the General Assembly may enact laws which provide that the findings of panels or commissions, selected and acting in accordance with law for the adjustment or settlement of grievances or disputes or for collective bargaining between policemen and firemen and their public employers shall be binding upon all parties and shall constitute a mandate to the head of the political subdivision which is the employer or to the appropriate officer of the Commonwealth if the Commonwealth is the employer, with respect to matters which can be remedied by administrative action, and to the lawmaking body of such political subdivision or of the Commonwealth, with respect to matters which require legislative action, to take the action necessary to carry out such findings.

Certain Local and Special Laws
Section 32.

The General Assembly shall pass no local or special law in any case which has been or can be provided for by general law and specifically the General assembly shall not pass any local or special law.
1. Regulating the affairs of counties, cities, townships, wards, boroughs, or school districts.
2. Vacating roads, town plats, streets or alleys.
3. Locating or changing county seats, erecting new counties or changing county lines.
4. Erecting new townships or boroughs, changing township lines, borough limits or school districts.
5. Remitting fines, penalties and forfeitures, or refunding moneys legally paid into the treasury.
6. Exempting property from taxation.
7. regulating labor, trade, mining or manufacturing.
8. Creating corporations, or amending, renewing or extending the charters thereof.
Nor shall the General Assembly indirectly enact any special or local law by the partial repeal of a general law; but laws repealing local or special acts may be passed.

Article IV

THE EXECUTIVE

Executive Department
Section 1.

The Executive Department of this Commonwealth shall consist of a Governor, Lieutenant Governor, Attorney General, Auditor General, State Treasurer, and Superintendent of Public Instruction and such other officers as the General Assembly may from time to time prescribe.

Duties of Governor; Election Procedure; Tie or contest

Section 2.

The supreme executive power shall be vested in the Governor, who shall take care that the laws be faithfully executed; he shall be chosen on the day of the general election, by the qualified electors of the Commonwealth, at the places where they shall vote for Representatives. The returns of every election for Governor shall be sealed up and transmitted to the seat of government, directed to the President of the Senate, who shall open and publish them in the presence of the members of both Houses of the General Assembly. The person having the highest number of votes shall be Governor, but if two or more be equal and highest in votes, one of them shall be chosen Governor by the joint vote of the members of both Houses. Contested elections shall be determined by a committee, to be selected from both Houses of the General Assembly, and formed and regulated in such manner as shall be directed by law. General Assembly. The person having the highest number of votes shall be Governor, but if two or more be equal and highest in votes, one of them shall be chosen Governor by the joint vote of members of both Houses. Contested elections shall be determined by a committee, to be selected from both Houses of the General Assembly, and formed and regulated in such manner as shall be directed by law.

Terms of Office of Governor; Number of Terms
Section 3.

The Governor shall hold his office during four years from the third Tuesday of January new ensuing his election. Except for the Governor who may be in office when this amendment is adopted, he shall be eligible to succeed himself for one additional term.

Lieutenant Governor
Section 4.

A Lieutenant Governor shall be chosen jointly with the Governor by the casting by each voter of a single vote applicable to both offices, for the same term, and subject to the same provisions as the Governor; he shall be President of the Senate. As such, he may vote in case of a tie on any question except the final passage of a bill or joint resolution, the adoption of a conference report or the concurrence in amendments made by the House of Representatives.

Attorney General
Section 4.

1. An Attorney General shall be chosen by the qualified electors of the Commonwealth on the day the general election is held for the Auditor General and State Treasurer; he shall hold his office during four years from the third Tuesday of January next ensuing his election and shall not be eligible to serve continuously for more than two successive terms; he shall be the chief law officer of the Commonwealth and shall exercise such powers and perform such duties as may be imposed by law.

Qualifications of Governor, Lieutenant Governor and Attorney General
Section 5.

No person shall be eligible to the office of Governor, Lieutenant Governor or Attorney General except a citizen of the United States, who shall have attained the age of thirty years, and have been seven years next preceding his election an inhabitant of this Commonwealth, unless he shall have been absent on the public business of the United States or of this Commonwealth. No person shall be eligible to the office of Attorney General except a member of the bar of the Supreme Court of Pennsylvania.

Disqualification for Offices of Governor, Lieutenant Governor and Attorney General
Section 6.

No member of Congress or person holding any office (except of attorney-at-law or in the National Guard or in a reserve component of the armed forces of the United States) under the United States or this Commonwealth shall exercise the office of Governor, Lieutenant Governor or Attorney General.

Military Power
Section 7.

The Governor shall be commander-in-chief of the military forces of the Commonwealth, except when they shall be called into actual service of the United States.

Appointing Power
Section 8.

(a) The Governor shall appoint a Secretary of Education and such other officers as he shall be authorized by law to appoint. The appointment of the Secretary of Education and of such other officers as may be specified by law, shall be subject to the consent of two-thirds or a majority of the members elected to the Senate as is specified by law.

(b) The Governor shall fill vacancies in offices to which he appoints by nominating to the Senate a proper person to fill the vacancy within 90 days of the first day of the vacancy and not thereafter. The Senate shall act on each executive nomination within 25 legislative days of its submission. If the Senate has not voted upon a nomination within 15 legislative days following such submission, any five members of the Senate may, in writing, request the presiding officer of the Senate to place the nomination before the entire Senate body whereby the nomination must be voted upon prior to the expiration of five legislative days or 25 legislative days following submission by the Governor, whichever occurs first. If the nomination is made during a recess or after adjournment sine die, the Senate shall act upon it within 25 legislative days after its return or reconvening. If the Senate for any reason fails to act upon a nomination submitted to it within the required 25 legislative days, the nominee shall take office as if the appointment had been consented to by the Senate. The Governor shall in a similar manner fill vacancies in the offices of Auditor General, State Treasurer, justice, judge, justice of the peace and in any other elective office he is authorized to fill. In the case of a vacancy in an elective office, a person shall be elected to the office on the next election day appropriate to the office unless the first day of the vacancy is within two calendar months immediately preceding the election day in which case the election shall be held on the second succeeding election day appropriate to the office.

(c) In acting on executive nominations, the Senate shall sit with open doors. The votes shall be taken by yeas and nays and shall be entered on the journal.

Pardoning Power; Board of Pardons
Section 9.

(a) In all criminal cases except impeachment the Governor shall have power to remit fines and forfeitures, to grant reprieves, commutation of sentences and pardons; but no pardon shall be granted, nor sentence commuted, except on the recommendation in writing of a majority of the Board of Pardons, and, in the case of a sentence of death or life imprisonment, on the unanimous recommendation in writing of the Board of Pardons, after full hearing in open session, upon due public notice. The recommendation, with the reasons therefor at length, shall be delivered to the Governor and a copy thereof shall be kept on file in the office of the Lieutenant Governor in a docket kept for that purpose.

(b) The Board of Pardons shall consist of the Lieutenant Governor who shall be chairman, the Attorney General and three members appointed by the Governor with the consent of a majority of the members elected to the Senate for terms of six years. The three members appointed by the Governor shall be residents of Pennsylvania. One shall be a crime victim, one a corrections expert and the third a doctor of medicine, psychiatrist or psychologist. The board shall keep records of its actions, which shall at all times be open for public inspection.]

Information from Department Officials
Section 10.

The Governor may require information in writing from the officers of the Executive Department, upon any subject relating to the duties of their respective offices.

Messages to the General Assembly
Section 11.

He shall, from time to time, give to the General Assembly information of the state of the Commonwealth, and recommend to their consideration such measures as he may judge expedient.

Power to Convene and Adjourn the General Assembly
Section 12.

He may, on extraordinary occasions, convene the General Assembly, and in case of disagreement between the two Houses, with respect to the time of adjournment, adjourn them to such time as he shall think proper, not exceeding four months. He shall have power to convene the Senate in extraordinary session by proclamation for the transaction of Executive business.

When Lieutenant Governor to Act as Governor
Section 13.

In the case of the death, conviction on impeachment, failure to qualify or resignation of the Governor, the Lieutenant Governor shall become Governor for the remainder of the term and in the case of the disability of the Governor, the powers, duties and emoluments of the office shall devolve upon the Lieutenant Governor until the disability is removed.

Vacancy in Office of Lieutenant Governor
Section 14.

In case of the death, conviction on impeachment, failure to qualify or resignation of the Lieutenant Governor, or in case he should become Governor under section 13 of this article, the President pro tempore of the Senate shall become Lieutenant Governor for the remainder of the term. In case of the disability of the Lieutenant Governor, the powers, duties and emoluments of the office shall devolve upon the President pro tempore of the Senate until the disability is removed. Should there be no Lieutenant Governor, the President pro tempore of the Senate shall become Governor if a vacancy shall occur in the office of Governor and in case of the disability of the Governor, the powers, duties and emoluments of the office shall devolve upon the President pro tempore of the Senate until the disability is removed. His seat as Senator shall become vacant whenever he shall become Governor and shall be filled by election as any other vacancy in Senate.

Approval of Bills; Vetoes
Section 15.

Every bill which shall have passed both Houses shall be presented to the Governor; if he approves he shall sign it, but if he shall not approve he shall return it with his objections to the House in which it shall have originated, which House shall enter the objections at large upon their journal, and proceed to re-consider it. If after such re-consideration, two-thirds of all the members elected to that House shall agree to pass the bill, it shall be sent with the objections to the other House by which likewise it shall be re-considered, and if approved by two-thirds of all the members elected to that House it shall be a law; but in such cases the votes of both Houses shall be determined by yeas and nays, and the names of the members voting for and against the bill shall be entered on the journals of each House, respectively. If any bill shall not be returned by the Governor within ten days after it shall have been presented to him, the same shall be a law in like manner as if he had signed it, unless the General Assembly, by their adjournment, prevent its return, in which case it shall be a law, unless he shall file the same, with his objections, in the office of the Secretary of the Commonwealth, and give notice thereof by public proclamation within thirty days after such adjournment.

Partial Disapproval of Appropriation Bills
Section 16.

The Governor shall have power to disapprove of any item of any bill, making appropriations of money, embracing distinct items, and the part or parts of the bill approved shall be the law, and the item or items of appropriation disapproved shall be void, unless re-passed according to the rules and limitations prescribed for the passage of other bills over the Executive veto.

Contested Elections of Governor, Lieutenant Governor and Attorney General; When Succeeded
Section 17.

The Chief Justice of the Supreme Court shall preside upon the trial of any contested election of Governor, Lieutenant Governor or Attorney General and shall decide questions regarding the admissibility of evidence, and shall, upon request of the committee, pronounce his opinion upon other questions of law involved in the trial. The Governor, Lieutenant Governor and Attorney General shall exercise the duties of their respective offices until their successors shall be duly qualified.

Terms of Office of Auditor General and State Treasurer; Number of Terms; Eligibility of State Treasurer to become Auditor General
Section 18.

The terms of the Auditor General and of the State Treasurer shall each be four years from the third Tuesday of January next ensuing his election. They shall be chosen by the qualified electors of the Commonwealth at general elections but shall not be eligible to serve continuously for more than two successive terms. The State Treasurer shall not be eligible to the office of Auditor General until fours years after he has been State Treasurer.

State Seal; Commissions
Section 19.

The present Great Seal of Pennsylvania shall be the seal of the State. All commissions shall be in the name and by authority of the Commonwealth of Pennsylvania, and be sealed with the State seal and signed by the Governor.

Article V

THE JUDICIARY

Unified Judicial System
Section 1.

The judicial power of the Commonwealth shall be vested in a unified judicial system consisting of the Supreme Court, the Superior Court, the Commonwealth Court, courts of common pleas, community courts, municipal and traffic courts in the City of Philadelphia, such other courts as may be provided by law and justices of the peace. All courts and justices of the peace and their jurisdiction shall be in this unified judicial system.

Supreme Court
Section 2.

The Supreme Court

(a) shall be the highest court of the Commonwealth and in this court shall be reposed the supreme judicial power of the Commonwealth;

(b) shall consist of seven justices, one of whom shall be the Chief ustice; and

(c) shall have such jurisdiction as shall be provided by law.

Superior Court
Section 3.

The Superior Court shall be a statewide court, and shall consist of the number of judges, which shall be not less than seven judges, and have such jurisdiction as shall be provided by this Constitution or by the General Assembly. One of its judges shall be the president judge.

Commonwealth Court

Section 4.

The Commonwealth Court shall be a statewide court, and shall consist of the number of judges and have such jurisdiction as shall be provided by law. One of its judges shall be the president judge.

Courts of Common Pleas
Section 5.

There shall be one court of common pleas for each judicial district

(a) having such divisions and consisting of such number of judges as shall be provided by law, one of whom shall be the president judge; and

(b) having unlimited original jurisdiction in all cases except as may otherwise be provided by law.

Community Courts; Philadelphia Municipal Court and Traffic Court
Section 6.

(a) in any judicial district a majority of the electors voting thereon may approve the establishment or discontinuance of a community court. Where a community court is approved, one community court shall be established; its divisions, number of judges and jurisdiction shall be as provided by law.

(b) The question whether a community court shall be established or discontinued in any judicial district shall be placed upon the ballot in a primary election by petition which shall be in the form prescribed by the officer of the Commonwealth who under law shall have supervision over elections. The petition shall be filed with that officer and shall be signed by a number of electors equal to five percent of the total votes cast for all candidates for the office occupied by a single official for which the highest number of votes was cast in that judicial district at the last preceding general or municipal election. The manner of signing such petitions, the time of circulating them, the affidavits of the persons circulating them and all other details not contained herein shall be governed by the general laws relating to elections. The question shall not be placed upon the ballot in a judicial district more than once in any five-year period.

(c) In the City of Philadelphia there shall be a municipal Court and a traffic court. The number of judges and the jurisdiction of each shall be as provided by law. These courts shall exist so long as a community court has not been established or in the event one has been discontinued under this section.

Justices of the Peace; Magisterial Districts
Section 7.

(a) In any judicial district, other than the City of Philadelphia, where a community court has not been established or where one has been discontinued there shall be one justice of the peace in each magisterial district. The jurisdiction of the justice of the peace shall be as provided by law.

(b) The General Assembly shall by law establish classes of magisterial districts solely on the basis of population and population density and shall fix the salaries to be paid justices of the peace in each class. The number and boundaries of magisterial districts of each class within each judicial district shall be established by the Supreme Court or by the courts of common pleas under the direction of the Supreme Court as required for the efficient administration of justice within each magisterial district.

Other Courts
Section 8.

The General Assembly may establish additional courts or divisions of existing courts, as needed, or abolish any statutory court or division thereof.

Right of Appeal
Section 9.

There shall be a right of appeal in all cases to a court of record from a court not of record; and there shall also be a right of appeal from a court of record or from an administrative agency to a court of record or to an appellate court, the selection of such court to be as provided by law; and there shall be such other rights of appeal as may be provided by law.

Judicial Administration
Section 10.

(a) The Supreme Court shall exercise general supervisory and administrative authority over all the courts and justices of the peace, including authority to temporarily assign judges and justices of the peace from one court or district to another as it deems appropriate.

(b) The Supreme Court shall appoint a court administrator and may appoint such subordinate administrators and staff as may be necessary and proper for the prompt and proper disposition of the business of all courts and justices of the peace.

(c) The Supreme Court shall have the power to prescribe general rules governing practice, procedure and the conduct of all courts, justices of the peace and all officers serving process or enforcing orders, judgments or decrees of any court or justice of the peace, including the power to provide for assignments and reassignment of classes of actions or classes of appeals among the several courts as the needs of justice shall require, and for admission to the bar and to practice law, and the administration of all courts and supervision of all officers of the Judicial Branch, if such rules are consistent with this Constitution and neither abridge, enlarge nor modify the substantive rights of any litigant, nor affect the right of the General Assembly to determine the jurisdiction of any court or justice of the peace, nor suspend nor alter any statute of limitation or repose. All laws shall be suspended to the extent that they are inconsistent with rules prescribed under these provisions. Notwithstanding the provisions of this section, the General Assembly may by statute provide for the manner of testimony of child victims or child material witnesses in criminal procedings, including the use of videotaped depositions or testimony by closed-circuit television.

(d) The Chief Justice and president judges of all courts with seven or less judges shall be the justice or judge longest in continuous service on their respective courts; and in the event of his resignation from this position the justice or judge next longest in continuous service shall be the Chief Justice or president judge. The president judges of all other courts shall be selected for five-year terms by the members of their respective courts, except that the president judge of the traffic court in the City of Philadelphia shall be appointed by the Governor. A chief Justice or president judge may resign such position and remain a member of the court. In the event of a tie vote for office of president judge in a court which elects its president judge, the Supreme Court shall appoint as president judge one of the judges receiving the highest number of votes.

(e) Should any two or more justices or judges of the same court assume office at the same time, they shall cast lots forthwith for priority of commission, and certify the results to the Governor who shall issue their commissions accordingly.

Judicial Districts; Boundaries
Section 11.

The number and boundaries of judicial districts shall be changed by the General Assembly only with the advice and consent of the Supreme Court.

Qualifications of Justices, Judges and Justices of the Peace
Section 12.

(a) Justices, judges and justices of the peace shall be citizens of the Commonwealth. Justices and judges, except the judges of traffic court in the City of Philadelphia, shall be members of the bar of the Supreme Court. Justices and judges of statewide courts, for a period of one year preceding their election or appointment and during their continuance in office, shall reside within the Commonwealth. Other judges and justices of the peace, for a period of one year preceding their election or appointment and during their continuance in office, shall reside with their respective districts, except as provided in this article for temporary assignments.

(b) Judges of the traffic court in the City of Philadelphia and justices of the peace shall be members of the bar of the Supreme Court or shall complete a course of training and instruction in the duties of their respective offices and pass an examination prior to assuming office. Such courses and examinations shall be as provided by law.

Election of Justices, Judges and Justices of the Peace; Vacancies
Section 13.

(a) Justices, judges and justices of the peace shall be elected at the municipal election next preceding the commencement of their respective terms of office by the electors of the Commonwealth or the respective districts in which they are to serve.

(b) A vacancy in the office of justice, judge or justice of the peace shall be filled by appointment by the Governor. The appointment shall be with the advice and consent of two-thirds of the members elected to the Senate, except in the case of justices of the peace which shall be by a majority. The person so appointed shall serve for a term ending on the first Monday of January following the next municipal election more than ten months after the vacancy occurs or for the remainder of the unexpired term whichever is less, except in the case of persons selected as additional judges to the Superior Court, where the General Assembly may stagger and fix the length of the initial terms of such additional judges by reference to any of the first, second and third municipal elections more than ten months after the additional judges are selected. The manner by which any additional judges are selected shall be provided by this section for the filling of vacancies in judicial offices.

(c) The provisions of section thirteen (b) shall not apply either in the case of a vacancy to be filled by retention election as provided in section fifteen (b), or in the case of a vacancy created by failure of a justice or judge to file a declaration for retention election as provided in section fifteen

(b) in the case of a vacancy occurring at the expiration of an appointive term under section thirteen (b), the vacancy shall be filled by election as provided in section thirteen (a).

(d) At the primary election in 1969, the electors of the Commonwealth may elect to have the justices and judges of the Supreme, Superior, Commonwealth and all other statewide courts appointed by the Governor from a list of persons qualified for the offices submitted to him by the Judicial Qualifications Commission. If a majority vote of those voting on the question is in favor of this method of appointment, then whenever any vacancy occurs thereafter for any reason in such court, the Governor shall fill the vacancy by appointment in the manner prescribed in this subsection. Such appointment shall not require the consent of the Senate.

(e) Each justice or judge appointed by the Governor under section thirteen

(d) shall hold office for an initial term ending the first Monday of January following the next municipal election more than twenty-four months following the appointment.

Judicial Qualifications Commission
Section 14.

(a) Should the method of judicial selection be adopted as provided in section thirteen (d), there shall be a Judicial Qualifications Commission, composed of four non-lawyer electors appointed by the Governor and three non-judge members of the bar of the Supreme Court appointed by the Supreme Court. No more than four members shall be of the same political party. The members of the commission shall serve for terms of seven years, with one member being selected each year. The commission shall consider all names submitted to it and recommend to the Governor not fewer than ten nor more than twenty of those qualified for each vacancy to be filled.

(b) During his term, no member shall hold a public office or public appointment for which he receive compensation, nor shall he hold office in a political party or political organization.

(c) A vacancy on the commission shall be filled by the appointment authority for the balance of the term.

Tenure of Justices, Judges and Justices of the Peace
Section 15.

(a) The regular term of office of justices and judges shall be ten years and the regular term of office for judges of the municipal court and traffic court in the City of Philadelphia and of justices of the peace shall be six years. The tenure of any justice or judge shall not be affected by changes in judicial districts or by reduction in the number of judges.

(b) A justice or judge elected under section thirteen (a), appointed under section thirteen (d) or retained under this section fifteen (b) may file a declaration of candidacy for retention election with the officer of the Commonwealth who under law shall have supervision over elections on or before the first Monday of January of the year preceding the year in which his term of office expires. If no declaration of candidacy for retention election with the officer of the Commonwealth who under law shall have supervision over elections on or before the first Monday of January of the year preceding the year in which his term of office expires. If no declaration is filed, a vacancy shall exist upon the expiration of the term of office of such justice of judge, to be filled by election under section thirteen (a) or by appointment under section thirteen (d) if applicable. If a justice or judge files a declaration, his name shall be submitted to the electors without party designation, on a separate judicial ballot or in a separate column on voting machines, at the municipal election immediately preceding the expiration of the term of office of the justice or judge, to determine only the question whether he shall be retained in office. If a majority is against retention, a vacancy shall exist upon the expiration of his term of office, to be filled by appointment under section thirteen (b) or under section thirteen (d) if applicable. If a majority favors retention, the justice or judge shall serve for the regular term of office provided herein, unless sooner removed or retired. At the expiration of each term a justice or judge shall be eligible for retention as provided herein subject only to the retirement provisions of this article.

Compensation and Retirement of Justices, Judges and Justices of the Peace
Section 16.

(a) Justices, judges and justices of the peace shall be compensated by the Commonwealth as provided by law. Their compensation shall not be diminished during their terms of office, unless by law applying generally to all salaried officers of the Commonwealth.

(b) Justices, judges and justices of the peace shall be retired on the last day of the calendar year in which they attain the age of 70 years. Former and retired justices, judges and justices of the peace shall receive such compensation as shall be provided by law. Except as provided by law, no salary, retirement benefit or other compensation, present or deferred, shall be paid to any justice, judge or justice of the peace who, under section 18 or under Article VI, is suspended, removed or barred from holding judicial office for conviction of a felony or misconduct in office or conduct which prejudices the proper administration of justice or brings the judicial office into disrepute.

(c) A former or retired justice or judge may, with his consent, be assigned by the Supreme Court on temporary judicial service as may be prescribed by rule of the Supreme Court.

Prohibited Activities
Section 17.

(a) Justices and judges shall devote full time to their judicial duties, and shall not engage in the practice of law, hold office in a political party or political organization, or hold an office or position of profit in the government of the United States, the Commonwealth or any municipal corporation or political subdivision thereof, except in the armed service of the United States or the Commonwealth.

(b) Justices and judges shall not engage in any activity prohibited by law and shall not violate any canon of legal or judicial ethics prescribed by the Supreme Court. Justices of the peace shall be governed by rules or canons which shall be prescribed by the Supreme Court.

(c) No justice, judge or justice of the peace shall be paid or accept for the performance of any judicial duty or for any service connected with his office, any fee, emolument of perquisite other than the salary and expenses provided by law.

(d) No duties shall be imposed by law upon the Supreme Court or any of the justices thereof or the Superior Court or any of the judges thereof, except such as are judicial, nor shall any of them exercise any power of appointment except as provided in this Constitution.

Suspension, Removal, Discipline and Compulsory Retirement
Section 18.

(a) There shall be an independent board within the Judicial Branch, known as the Judicial Conduct Board, the composition, powers and duties of which shall be as follows:

(1) The board shall be composed of 12 members, as follows: two judges, other than senior judges, one from the courts of common pleas and the other from either the Superior Court or the Commonwealth Court, one justice of the peace who need not be a member of the bar of the Supreme Court, three non-judge members of the bar of the Supreme Court and six non-lawyer electors.

(2) The judge from either the Superior Court or the Commonwealth Court, the justice of the peace, one non-judge member of the bar of the Supreme Court and three non-lawyer electors shall be appointed to the board by the Supreme Court. The judge from the courts of common pleas, two nonjudge members of the bar of the Supreme Court and three non-lawyer electors shall be appointed to the board by the Governor.

(3) Except for the initial appointees whose terms shall be provided by the schedule to this article, the members shall serve for terms of four years. All members must be residents of this Commonwealth. No more than three of the six members appointed by the Supreme Court may be registered in the same political party. No more than three of the six members appointed by the Governor may be registered in the same political party. Membership of a judge or justice of the peace shall terminate if the member ceases to hold the judicial position that qualified the member for the appointment. Membership shall terminate if a member attains a position that would have rendered the member ineligible for appointment at the time of the appointment. A vacancy shall be filled by the respective appointing authority for the remainder of the term to which the member was appointed. No member may serve more than four consecutive years but may be reappointed after a lapse of one year. The Governor shall convene the board for its first meeting. At that meeting and annually thereafter, the members of the board shall elect a chairperson. The board shall act only with the concurrence of a majority of its members.

(4) No member of the board, during the member's term, may hold office in a political party or political organization. Except for a judicial member, no member of the board, during the member's term, may hold a compensated public office or public appointment. All members shall be reimbursed for expenses necessarily incurred in the discharge of their official duties.

(5) The board shall prescribe general rules governing the conduct of members. A member may be removed by the board for a violation of the rules governing the conduct of members.

(6) The board shall appoint a chief counsel and other staff, prepare and administer its own budget as provided by law, exercise supervisory and administrative authority over all board staff and board functions, establish and promulgate its own rules of procedure, prepare and disseminate an annual report and take other actions as are necessary to ensure its efficient operation. The budget request of the board shall be made by the board as a separate item in the request submitted by the Supreme Court on behalf of the Judicial Branch to the General Assembly.

(7) The board shall receive and investigate complaints regarding judicial conduct filed by individuals or initiated by the board, issue subpoenas to compel testimony under oath of witnesses, including the subject of the investigation, and to compel the production of documents, books, accounts and other records relevant to the investigation-, determine whether there is probable cause to file formal charges against a justice. judge or justice of the peace for conduct proscribed by this section; and present the case in support of the charges before the Court of Judicial Discipline.

(8) Complaints filed with the board or initiated by the board shall not be public information. Statements, testimony, documents, records or other information or evidence acquired by the board in the conduct of an investigation shall not be public information. A justice, judge or justice of the peace who is the subject of a complaint filed with the board or initiated by the board or of an investigation conducted by the board shall be apprised of the nature and content of the complaint and afforded an opportunity to respond fully to the complaint prior to any probable cause determination by the board. All proceedings of the board shall be confidential except when the subject of the investigation waives confidentiality. If, independent of any action by the board, the fact that an investigation by the board is in progress becomes a matter of public record, the

board may, at the direction of the subject of the investigation, issue a statement to confirm-n that the investigation is in progress, to clarify the procedural aspects of the proceedings, to explain the rights of the subject of the investigation to a fair hearing without prejudgment or to provide the response of the subject of the investigation to the complaint. In acting to dismiss a complaint for lack of probable cause to file formal charges, the board may, at its discretion, issue a statement or report to the complainant or to the subject of the complaint, which may contain the identity of the complainant, the identity of the subject of the complaint, (lie contents and nature of the complaint, the actions taken in the conduct of the investigation and the results and conclusions of the investigation. Tile board may include with a report a copy of information or evidence acquired in the course of the investigation.

(9) If the board finds probable cause to file formal charges concerning mental or physical disability against a justice, judge or justice of the peace, the board shall so notify the subject of the charges and provide the subject with an opportunity to resign from judicial office or, when appropriate, to enter a rehabilitation program prior to the filing of the formal charges with the Court of Judicial Discipline.

(10) Members of the board and its chief counsel and staff shall be absolutely immune from suit for all conduct in the course of their official duties. No civil action or disciplinary complaint predicated upon the filing of a complaint or other documents with the board or testimony before the board may be maintained against any complainant, witness or counsel.

(b) There shall be a Court of Judicial Discipline, the composition, powers and duties of which shall be as follows:

(1) The court shall be composed of a total of eight members as follows: three judges other than senior judges from the courts of common pleas, die Superior Court or the Commonwealth Court, one justice of the peace, two non-judge members of the bar of the Supreme Court and two non-lawyer electors. Two judges, the justice of the peace and one non-lawyer elector shall be appointed to the court by the Supreme Court. One judge, the two non-judge members of the bar of the Supreme Court and one non-lawyer elector shall be appointed to the court by the Governor.

(2) Except for the initial appointees whose terms shall be provided by the schedule to this article, each member shall serve for a term of four years; however, the member, rather than the member's successor, shall continue to participate in any hearing in progress at the end of the member's term. All members must be residents of this Commonwealth. No more than two of the members appointed by the Supreme Court may be registered in the same political party. No more than two of the members appointed by the Governor may be registered in the same political party. Membership of a judge or justice of the peace shall terminate if the judge or justice of the peace ceases to hold the judicial position that qualified the judge or justice of the peace for appointment. Membership shall terminate if a member attains a position that would have rendered that person ineligible for appointment at the time of the appointment. A vacancy on the court shall be filled by the respective appointing authority for the remainder of the term to which the member was appointed in the same manner in which the original appointment occurred. No member of the court may serve more than four consecutive years but may be reappointed after a lapse of one year.

(3) The court shall prescribe general rules governing the conduct of members. A member may be removed by the court for a violation of the rules of conduct prescribed by the court. No member, during the member's term of service, may hold office in any political party or political organization. Except for a judicial member, no member of the court, during the member's term of service, may hold a compensated public office or public appointment. All members of the court shall be reimbursed for expenses necessarily incurred in the discharge of their official duties.

(4) The court shall appoint staff and prepare and administer its own budget as provided by law and undertake actions needed to ensure its efficient operation. All actions of the court, including disciplinary action, shall require approval by a majority vote of the members of the court. The

budget request of the court shall be made as a separate item in the request by the Supreme Court on behalf of the Judicial Branch to the General Assembly. The court shall adopt rules to govern the conduct of proceedings before the court.

(5) Upon the filing of formal charges with the court by the board, the court shall promptly schedule a hearing or hearings to determine whether a sanction should be imposed against a justice, judge or justice of the peace pursuant to the provisions of this section. The court shall be a court of record, with all the attendant duties and powers appropriate to its function. Formal charges filed with the court shall be a matter of public record. All hearings conducted by the court shall be public proceedings conducted pursuant to the rules adopted by the court and in accordance with the principles of due process and the law of evidence. Parties appearing before the court shall have a right to discovery pursuant to the rules adopted by the court and shall have the right to subpoena witnesses and to compel the production of documents. books, accounts and other records as relevant. The subject of the charges shall be presumed innocent in any proceeding before (fie court. and the board shall have the burden of proving the charges by clear and convincing evidence. All decisions of the court shall be in writing and shall contain findings of fact and conclusions of law. A decision of the court may order removal from office, suspension, censure or other discipline as authorized by this section and as warranted by the record.

(6) Members of the court and the court's staff shall be absolutely immune from suit for all conduct in the course of their official duties, and no civil action or disciplinary complaint predicated on testimony before the court may be maintained against any witness or counsel.

(c) Decisions of the court shall be subject to review as follows:

(1) A justice, judge or justice of the peace shall have the right to appeal a final adverse order of discipline of the court. A judge or justice of the peace shall have the right to appeal to the Supreme Court in a manner consistent with rules adopted by the Supreme Court; a justice shall have the right to appeal to a special tribunal composed of seven judges, other than senior judges, chosen by lot from the judges of the Superior Court and Commonwealth Court who do not sit on the Court of Judicial Discipline or the board, in a manner consistent with rules adopted by the Supreme Court. The special tribunal shall hear and decide the appeal in the same manner in which the Supreme Court would hear and decide an appeal from an order of the court.

(2) On appeal, the Supreme Court or special tribunal shall review the record of the proceedings of the court as follows: on the law, the scope of review is plenary; on the facts, the scope of review is clearly erroneous; and, as to sanctions, the scope of review is whether the sanctions imposed were lawful. The Supreme Court or special tribunal may revise or reject an order of the court upon a determination that the order did not sustain this standard of review; otherwise, the Supreme Court or special tribunal shall affirm the order of the court.

(3) An order of the court which dismisses a complaint against a judge or justice of the peace may be appealed by the board to the Supreme Court, but the appeal shall be limited to questions of law. An order of the court which dismisses a complaint against a justice of the Supreme Court may be appealed by the board to a special tribunal in accordance with paragraph (1), but the appeal shall be limited to questions of law.

(4) No justice, judge or justice of the peace may participate as a member of the board, the court, a special tribunal or the Supreme Court in any proceeding in which the justice, judge or justice of the peace is a complainant, the subject of a complaint, a party or a witness.

(d) A justice, judge or justice of the peace shall be subject to disciplinary action pursuant to this section as follows:

(1) A justice, judge or justice of the peace may be suspended, removed from office or otherwise

disciplined for conviction of a felony; violation of section 17 of this article; misconduct in office; neglect or failure to perform the duties of office or conduct which prejudices the proper administration of justice or brings the judicial office into disrepute, whether or not the conduct occurred while acting in a judicial capacity or is prohibited by law; or conduct in violation of a canon or rule prescribed by the Supreme Court. In the case of a mentally or physically disabled justice, judge or justice of the peace, the court may enter an order of removal from office, retirement, suspension or other limitations on the activities of the justice, judge or justice of the peace as warranted by the record. Upon a final order of the court for suspension without pay or removal, prior to any appeal, the justice, judge or justice of the peace shall be suspended or removed from office; and the salary of the justice, judge or justice of the peace shall cease from the date of the order.

(2) Prior to a hearing, the court may issue an interim order directing the suspension, with or without pay, of any justice, judge or justice of the peace against whom formal charges have been filed with the court by the board or against whom has been filed an indictment or information charging a felony. An interim order under this paragraph shall not be considered a final order from which an appeal may be taken.

(3) A justice, judge or justice of the peace convicted of misbehavior in office by a court, disbarred as a member of the bar of the Supreme Court or removed under this section shall forfeit automatically his judicial office and thereafter be ineligible for judicial office.

(4) A justice, judge or justice of the peace who files for nomination for or election to any public office other than a judicial office shall forfeit automatically his judicial office.

(5) This section is in addition to and not in substitution for the provisions for impeachment for misbehavior in office contained in Article VI. No justice, judge or justice of the peace against whom impeachment proceedings are pending in the Senate shall exercise any of the duties of office until acquittal.

COURTS OTHER THAN IN THE CITY OF PHILADELPHIA AND ALLEGHENY COUNTY

The Supreme Court
Section 1.

The Supreme Court shall exercise all the powers and, until otherwise provided by law, jurisdiction now vested in the present Supreme Court and, until otherwise provided by law, the accused in all cases of felonious homicide shall have the right of appeal to the Supreme Court.

The Superior Court
Section 2.

Until otherwise provided by law, the Superior Court shall exercise all the jurisdiction now vested in the present Superior Court. The present terms of all judges of the Superior Court which would otherwise expire on the first Monday of January in an odd-numbered year shall be extended to expire in the even- numbered year next following.

Commonwealth Court
Section 3.

The Commonwealth Court shall come into existence on January 1, 1970. Notwithstanding anything to the contrary in this article, the General Assembly shall stagger the initial terms of judges of the Commonwealth Court.

The Courts of Common Pleas
Section 4.

Until otherwise provided by law, the several courts of common pleas shall exercise the jurisdiction now vested in the present courts of common pleas. The courts of oyer and terminer and general jail delivery, quarter sessions of the peace, and orphans courts are abolished and the several courts of common pleas shall also exercise the jurisdiction of these courts. Orphans' courts in judicial districts having separate orphans' courts shall become orphans' court divisions of the courts of common pleas and the court of common pleas in those judicial districts shall exercise the jurisdiction presently exercised by the separate orphans' courts through their respective orphans' court division.

Orphans' Court Judges
Section 5.

In those judicial districts having separate orphans' courts, the present judges thereof shall become judges of the orphans' court division of the court of common pleas and the present president judge shall become the president judge of the orphans' court division of the court of common pleas for the remainder of his term without diminution in salary.

Courts of Common Pleas in Multi-County Judicial Districts
Section 6.

Courts of common pleas in multi-county judicial districts are abolished as separate courts and are hereby constituted as branches of the single court of common pleas established under this article in each such judicial district.

Community Courts
Section 7.

In a Judicial district which establishes a community court, a person serving as a justice of the peace at such time:

(a) May complete his term exercising the jurisdiction provided by law with the compensation provided by law, and

(b) Upon completion of his term, his office is abolished and no judicial function of the kind heretofore exercised by a justice of the peace shall thereafter be exercised other than by the community court.

JUSTICES, JUDGES AND JUSTICES OF THE PEACE

Justices, Judges and Justices of the Peace
Section 8.

Notwithstanding any provision in the article, a present justice, judge or justice of the peace may complete his term of office.

Associate Judges
Section 9.

The office of associate judge not learned in the law is abolished, but a present associate judge may complete his term.

Retention Election of Present Justices and Judges
Section 10.

A present judge who was originally elected to office and seeks retention in 1969 municipal election and is otherwise eligible may file his declaration of candidacy by February 1, 1969.

Selection of President Judges
Section 11.

(a) Except in the City of Philadelphia, section ten (d) of the article shall become effective upon the expiration of the term of the present president judge, or upon earlier vacancy.

(b) Notwithstanding section ten (d) of the article the president judge of the Superior Court shall be the judge longest in continuous service on such court if such judge was a member of such court on the first Monday of January 1977. If no such judge exists or is willing to serve as president judge shall be selected as provided by this article.

MAGISTRATES, ALDERMEN AND JUSTICES OF THE PEACE AND MAGISTERIAL DISTRICTS OTHER THAN IN THE CITY OF PHILADELPHIA

Magistrates, Aldermen and Justices of the Peace
Section 12.

An alderman, justice of the peace or magistrate:

(a) May complete his term, exercising the jurisdiction provided by law and with the method of compensation provided by law prior to the adoption of this article;

(b) Shall be deemed to have taken and passed the examination required by this article for justices of the peace if he has completed one full term of office before creation of a magisterial district, and

(c) At the completion of his term, his office is abolished.

(d) Except for officers completing their terms, after the first Monday in January, 1970, no judicial function of the kind heretofore exercised by these officers, by majors and like officers in municipalities shall be exercised by any officer other than the one justice of the peace elected or appointed to serve in that magisterial district.

Magisterial Districts
Section 13.

So that the provisions of this article regarding the establishment of magisterial districts and the instruction and examination of justices of the peace may be self-executing, until otherwise provided by law in a manner agreeable to this article, the following provisions shall be in force:

(a) The Supreme Court or the courts of common pleas under the direction of the Supreme Court shall fix the number and boundaries of magisterial districts of each class within each judicial district by January 1, 1969, and these magisterial districts, except where a community court has been adopted, shall come into existence on January 1, 1970, the justices of the peace thereof to be elected at the municipal election in 1969. These justices of the peace shall retain no fine, costs or any other sum that shall be delivered into their hands for the performance of any judicial duty or for any service connected with their offices, but shall remit the same to the Commonwealth, county, municipal subdivision, school district or otherwise as may be provided by law.

(b) Classes of magisterial districts.

(i) Magisterial districts of the first class shall have a population density of more than five thousand persons per square mile and a population of not less than sixty-five thousand persons.

(ii) Magisterial districts of the second class shall have a population density of between one thousand and five thousand persons per square mile and a population of between twenty thousand persons and sixty-five thousand persons.

(iii) Magisterial districts of the third class shall have a population density of between two hundred and one thousand persons per square mile and a population of between twelve thousand persons and twenty thousand persons.

(iv) Magisterial districts of the fourth class shall have a population density of between seventy and two hundred persons per square mile and a population of between seven thousand five hundred persons and twelve thousand persons.

(v) Magisterial districts of the fifth class shall have a population density of under seventy persons per square mile and a population of between four thousand persons and seven thousand five hundred persons.

(c) Salaries of justices of the peace. The salaries of the justices of the peace shall be as follows:

(i) In first class magisterial districts, twelve thousand dollars per year.

(ii) In second class magisterial districts, ten thousand dollars per year.

(iii) In third class magisterial districts, eight thousand dollars per year.

(iv) In fourth and fifth class magisterial districts, five thousand dollars per year.

(v) The salaries here fixed shall be paid by the State Treasurer and for such payment this article and schedule shall be sufficient warrant.

(d) Course of training, instruction and examination. The course of training and instruction and examination in civil and criminal law and procedure for a justice of the peace shall be devised by the Department of Public Instruction, and it shall administer this course and examination to insure that justices of the peace are competent to perform their duties.

Magisterial Districts
Section 14.

Effective immediately upon establishment of magisterial districts and until otherwise prescribed the civil and criminal procedural rules relating to venue shall apply to magisterial districts; all proceedings before aldermen, magistrates and justices of the peace shall be brought in and only in a magisterial district in which occurs an event which would give rise to venue in a court of record; the court of common pleas upon its own motion or on application at any stage of proceedings shall transfer any proceeding in any magisterial district to the justice of the peace for the magisterial district in which proper venue lies.

PROTHONOTARIES AND CLERKS OTHER THAN IN THE CITY OF PHILADELPHIA

Prothonotaries, Clerks of Courts, Clerks of Orphans' Courts
Section 15.

Until otherwise provided by law, the offices of prothonotary and clerk of courts shall become the offices of prothonotary and clerk of courts of the court of common pleas of the judicial district, and in multi-county judicial districts of their county's branch of the court of common pleas, and the clerk of the orphans' court in a judicial district now having a separate orphans' court shall become the clerk of the orphans' court division of the court of common pleas, and these officers shall continue to perform the duties of the office and to maintain and be responsible for the records, books and dockets as heretofore. In judicial districts where the clerk of the orphans' court is not the register of wills, he shall continue to perform the duties of the office and to maintain and be responsible for the records, books and dockets as heretofore until otherwise provided by law.

THE CITY OF PHILADELPHIA

Courts and Judges
Section 16.

Until otherwise provided by law:

(a) The court of common pleas shall consist of a trial division, orphans' court division and family court division.

(b) The judges of the court of common pleas shall become judges of the trial division of the court of common pleas provided for in this article and their tenure shall not otherwise be affected.

(c) The judges of the county court shall become judges of the family court division of the court of common pleas and their tenure shall not otherwise be affected.

(d) The judges of the orphans' court shall become judges of the orphans' court division of the court of common pleas and their tenure shall not otherwise be affected.

(e) As designated by the Governor, twenty-two of the present magistrates shall become judges of the municipal court and six shall become judges of the traffic court, and their tenure shall not otherwise be affected.

(f) One of the judges of the court of common pleas shall be president judge and he shall be selected in the manner provided in section ten (d) of this article. He shall be the administrative head of the court and shall supervise the court's judicial business.

(g) Each division of the court of common pleas shall be presided over by an administrative judge, who shall be one of its judges and shall be elected for a term of five years by a majority vote of the judges of that division. He shall assist the president judge in supervising the judicial business of the court and shall be responsible to him. Subject to the foregoing, the judges of the court of common pleas shall prescribe rules defining the duties of the administrative judges. The president judge shall have the power to assign judges from each division to each other division of court when required to expedite the business of the court.

(h) Until all members of the municipal court are members of the bar of the Supreme Court, the president judge of the court of common pleas shall appoint one of the judges of the municipal court as president judge for a five-year term or at the pleasure of the president judge of the court of common pleas. The president judge of the municipal court shall be eligible to succeed himself as president judge for any number of terms and shall be the administrative head of that court and shall supervise the judicial business of the court. He shall promulgate all administrative rules and regulations and make all judicial assignments. The president judge of the court of common pleas may assign temporarily judges of the municipal court who are members of the bar of the Supreme Court to the court of common pleas when required to expedite the business of the court.

(i) The Governor shall appoint one of the judges of the traffic court as president judge for a term of five years or at the pleasure to the Governor. The president judge of the traffic court shall be eligible to succeed himself as president judge for any number of terms, shall be the executive and administrative head of the traffic court, and shall supervise the judicial business of the court, shall promulgate all administrative rules and regulations, and shall make all judicial assignments.

(j) The exercise of all supervisory and administrative powers detailed in this section sixteen shall be subject to the supervisory and administrative control of the Supreme Court.

(k) The prothonotary shall continue to exercise the duties of that office for the trial division of the court of common pleas and for the municipal court.

(l) The clerk of quarter sessions shall continue to exercise the duties of that office for the trial division of the court of common pleas and for the municipal court.

(m) That officer serving as clerk to the county court shall continue to exercise the duties of that office for the family division of the court of common pleas.

(n) The register of wills shall serve ex officio as clerk of the orphans' court division of the court of common pleas.

(o) The court of common pleas shall have unlimited original jurisdiction in all cases except those cases assigned by this schedule to the municipal court and to the traffic court. The court of common pleas shall have all the jurisdiction now vested in the court of common pleas, the court of oyer and terminer and general jail delivery, courts of quarter sessions of the peace, orphans' court, and county court. Jurisdiction in all of the foregoing cases shall be exercised through the trial division of the court of common pleas except in those cases which are assigned by this schedule to the orphans' court and family court divisions of the court of common pleas. The court of common pleas through the trial division shall also hear and determine appeals from the municipal court and traffic court.

(p) The court of common pleas through the orphans' court division shall exercise the jurisdiction heretofore exercised by the orphans' court.

(q) The court of common pleas through the family court division of the court of common pleas shall exercise jurisdiction in the following matters:

(i) Domestic Relations: desertion or nonsupport of wives, children and indigent parents, including children born out of wedlock; proceedings for custody of children; divorce and annulment and property matters relating thereto.

(ii) Juvenile Matters: dependent, delinquent and neglected children and children under eighteen years of age, suffering from epilepsy, nervous or mental defects, incorrigible, runaway and disorderly minors eighteen to twenty years of age and preliminary hears in criminal cases where the victim is a juvenile.

(iii) Adoptions and Delayed Birth Certificates

(r) The municipal court shall have jurisdiction in the following matters.

(i) Committing magistrates' jurisdiction in all criminal matters.

(ii) All summary offenses, except those under the motor vehicle laws.

(iii) All criminal offenses for which no prison term may be imposed or which are punishable by a term of imprisonment of not more than two years, and indictable offenses under the motor vehicle laws for which no prison term may be imposed or punishable by a term of imprisonment of not more than three years. In these cases, the defendant shall have no right of trial by jury in that court, but he shall have the right of appeal for trial de novo including the right to trial by jury to the trial division of the court of common pleas. Until there are a sufficient number of judges who are members of the bar of the Supreme Court serving in the municipal court to handle such matters, the trial division of the court of common pleas shall have concurrent jurisdiction over such matters, the assignment of cases to the respective courts to be determined by rule prescribed by the president judge of the court of common pleas.

(iv) Matters arising under the Landlord and Tenant Act of 1951.

(v) All civil claims involving less than five hundred dollars. In these cases, the parties shall have no right of trial by jury in that court but shall have a right of appeal for a trial de novo including the right to trial by jury to the trial division of the court of common pleas, it being the purpose of this subsection to establish an expeditious small claims procedure whereby it shall not be necessary for the litigants to obtain council. This limited grant of civil jurisdiction shall be co-extensive with the civil jurisdiction of the trial division of the court of common pleas.

(vi) As commissioners to preside at arraignments, fix and accept bail, issue warrants and perform duties of a similar nature. The grant of jurisdiction under clauses (iii) and (v) of this subsection may be exercised only by those judges who are members of the bar of the Supreme Court.

(s) The traffic court shall have exclusive jurisdiction of all summary offenses under the motor vehicle laws.

(t) the courts of oyer and terminer and general jail delivery, quarter sessions of the peace, the county court, the orphans' court and the ten separate courts of common pleas are abolished and their jurisdiction and powers shall be exercised by the court of common pleas provided for in this article through the divisions established by this schedule.

(u) The office of magistrate, the board of magistrates and the present traffic court are abolished.

(v) Those judges appointed to the municipal court in accordance with subsection (e) of this section who are not members of the bar of the Supreme Court shall be eligible to complete their present terms and to be elected to and serve for one additional term, but not thereafter.

(w) The causes, proceedings, books, dockets and records of the abolished courts shall become those of the court or division thereof to which, under this schedule, jurisdiction of the proceedings or matters concerned has been transferred, and that court or division thereof shall determine and conclude such proceedings as if it had assumed jurisdiction in the first instance.

(x) The present president judges of the abolished courts and chief magistrate shall continue to receive the compensation to which they are now entitled as president judges and chief magistrate until the end of their present terms as president judges and chief magistrate respectively.

(y) The offices of prothonotary and register of wills in the City of Philadelphia shall no longer be considered constitutional offices under this article, but their powers and functions shall continue as at present until these offices are covered in the Home Rule Charter by a referendum in the manner provided by law.

(z) If a community court is established in the City of Philadelphia, a person serving as a judge of the municipal or traffic court at that time:

(i) Notwithstanding the provisions of subsection (v) of this section, may complete his term exercising the jurisdiction provided by law and with the compensation provided by law; and

(ii) At the completion of his term, his office is abolished and no jurisdiction of the kind exercised by those officers immediately after the effective date of this article and schedule shall thereafter be exercises other than by the community court.

ALLEGHENY COUNTY

Courts
Section 17.

Until otherwise provided by law:

(a) The court of common pleas shall consist of a trial division, an orphans' court division and a family court division; the courts of oyer and terminer and general jail delivery and quarter sessions of the peace, the county court, the orphans' court, and the juvenile court are abolished and their present jurisdiction shall be exercised by the court of common pleas. Until otherwise provided by rule of the court of common pleas and, except as otherwise provided in this schedule, the court of common pleas shall exercise the jurisdiction of the present court of common pleas and the present county court through the trial division. Until otherwise provided by rule of the court of common pleas, the jurisdiction of the present orphans' court, except as otherwise provided in this schedule, shall be exercised by the court of common pleas through the orphans' court division.

(b) Until otherwise provided by rule of the court of common pleas, the court of common pleas shall exercise jurisdiction in the following matters through the family court division:

(i) Domestic Relations: Desertion or nonsupport or nonsupport of wives, children and indigent parents, including children born out of wedlock; proceedings, including habeas corpus, for custody of children; divorce and annulment and property matters relating thereto.

(ii) Juvenile Matters: All matters now within the jurisdiction of the juvenile court.

(iii) Adoptions and Delayed Birth Certificates.

Judges
Section 18.

Until otherwise provided by law, the present judges of the court of common pleas shall continue to act as the judges of that court; the present judges of the county court shall become judges of the court of common pleas; the present judges of the orphans' court shall become judges of the orphans' court division of the court of common pleas; the present judges of the juvenile court shall become judges of the family court division of the court of common pleas.

President Judges
Section 19.

The present president judge of the court of common pleas may complete his term as president judge; the present president judge of the orphans' court shall be the president judge of the orphans' court division of the court of common pleas for the remainder of his term as president judge, and the present president judge of the county court shall be the president judge of the family court division of the court of common pleas for the remainder of his term as president judge, all these without diminution of salary as president judge. The president judge of the trial division shall be selected pursuant to section twenty of this schedule.

President Judges; Court Division
Section 20.

Until otherwise provided by law, the trial division, the orphans' court division and the family court division of the court of common pleas shall each be presided over by a president judge, who shall be one of the judges of such division and shall be elected for a term of five years by a majority vote of the judges of that division. He shall assist the president judge of the court of common pleas in supervising the judicial business of the court and shall be responsible to him. Subject to the foregoing, the judges of the court of common pleas shall prescribe rules defining the duties of the president judges. The president judge of the court of common pleas shall have the power to assign judges from one division to another division of the court when required to expedite the business of the court. The exercise of these supervisory and administrative powers, however, shall be subject to the supervisory and administrative powers of the Supreme Court.

THE CITY OF PITTSBURGH

Inferior Courts
Section 21.

Upon the establishment of magisterial districts pursuant to this article and schedule, and unless otherwise provided by law, the police magistrates, including those serving in the traffic court, the housing court and the city court shall continue as at present. Such magistrates shall be part of the unified judicial system and shall be subject to the general supervisory and administrative authority of the Supreme Court. Such magistrates shall be subject to the provisions of this article and schedule regarding educational requirements and prohibited activities of justices of the peace.

CAUSES, PROCEEDINGS, BOOKS AND RECORDS

Causes, Proceedings, Books and Records
Section 22.

All causes and proceedings pending in any abolished court or office of the justice of the peace shall be determined and concluded by the court to which jurisdiction of the proceedings has been transferred under this schedule and all books, dockets and records of any abolished court or office of the justice of the peace shall become those of the court to which, under this schedule, jurisdiction of the proceedings concerned has been transferred.

COMMISSION AND BOARD

Judicial Qualifications Commission
Section 23.

The selection of the first members of the Judicial Qualifications Commission provided for in section fourteen (a) of this article shall be made as follows: The Governor shall appoint the four non-lawyer members for terms of, respectively, one year, three years, five years and seven years, no more than two of whom shall be members of the same political party. The Supreme Court shall appoint the three non-judge members of the bar of the Supreme Court of Pennsylvania for terms, respectively, of two years, four years and six years, no more than two of whom shall be members of the same political party.

Judicial Inquiry and Review Board
Section 24.

[3] 24. Judicial discipline.

(a) The members of the Judicial Inquiry and Review Board shall vacate their offices 90 days after the adoption of the amendment to section 18 of this article, and all proceedings pending before the Judicial Inquiry and Review Board and all records shall be transferred to the Judicial Conduct

Board for further proceedings.

(b) Of the members initially appointed to the Judicial Conduct Board, the judge appointed by the Supreme Court shall serve a four-year term, and the judge appointed by the Governor shall serve a three-year ten-n. The justice of the peace initially appointed shall serve a two-year term. Of the three nonjudge members of the bar of the Supreme Court initially appointed, the first appointed by the Governor shall serve a three-year term, the next appointed by the Governor shall serve a two-year term, and the non-judge member of the bar of the Supreme Court appointed by the Supreme Court shall serve a one-year term. Of the six non-lawyer electors initially appointed, the first appointed by the Governor and the first appointed by the Supreme Court shall serve a four-year term, the next appointed by the Governor and the next appointed by the Supreme Court shall serve a three-year term, and the next appointed by the Governor and the next appointed by the Supreme Court shall serve a two-year term.

(c) Of the three judges initially appointed to the Court of Judicial Discipline, the first appointed by the Supreme Court shall serve a four-year term, the next appointed by the Supreme Court shall serve a three-year term, and the judge appointed by the Governor shall serve a two-year term. The justice of the peace initially appointed shall serve a one-year term. Of the non-judge members of the bar initially appointed, the first appointed shall serve a four-year term, and the next appointed shall serve a three-year term. Of the two non-lawyer electors initially appointed, the non-lawyer elector appointed by the Governor shall serve a three-year term, and the non-lawyer elector appointed by the Supreme Court shall serve a two-year term.

GENERAL PROVISIONS

Dispensing with Trial by Jury
Section 25.

Until otherwise provided by law, the parties, by agreement filed, may in any civil case dispense with trial by jury, and submit the decision of such case to the court having jurisdiction thereof, and such court shall hear and determine the same; and the judgment thereon shall be subject to writ of error as in other cases.

Writs of Certiorari
Section 26.

Unless and until changed by rule of the Supreme Court, in addition to the right of appear under section nine of this article, the judges of the courts of common pleas, within their respective judicial districts, shall have power to issue writs of certiorari to the municipal court in the City of Philadelphia, justices of the peace and inferior courts not of record and to cause their proceedings to be brought before them, and right and justice to be done.

Judicial Districts
Section 27.

Until changed in accordance with section eleven of this article, the number and boundaries of judicial districts shall remain as at present.

Referendum
Section 28.

The officer of the Commonwealth who under law shall have supervision over elections shall cause the question provided for in section thirteen (d) of this article to be placed on the ballot in the 1969 primary election throughout the Commonwealth.

Persons Specially Admitted by Local Rules
Section 29.

Any person now specially admitted to practice may continue to practice in the court of common pleas or in that division of the court of common pleas and the municipal court in the City of Philadelphia which substantially includes the practice for which such person was previously specially admitted.

Article VI

PUBLIC OFFICERS

Section of Officers Not Otherwise Provided for in Constitution
Section 1.

All officers, whose selection is not provided for in this Constitution, shall be elected or appointed as may be directed by law.

Incompatible Offices
Section 2.

No member of Congress from this State, nor any person holding or exercising any office or appointment of trust or profit under the United States, shall at the same time hold or exercise any office in this State to which a salary, fees or perquisites shall be attached. The General Assembly may be law declare what offices are incompatible.

Oath of Office
Section 3.

Senators, Representatives and all judicial, State and county officers shall, before entering on the duties of their respective offices, take and subscribe the following oath or affirmation before a person authorized to administer oaths. "I do solemnly swear (or affirm) that I will support, obey and defend the Constitution of the United States and the Constitution of this Commonwealth and that I will discharge the duties of my office with fidelity." The oath or affirmation shall be administered to a member of the Senate or to a member of the House of Representatives in the hall of the House to which he shall have been elected. Any person refusing to take the oath or affirmation shall forfeit his office.

Power of Impeachment
Section 4.

The House of Representatives shall have the sole power of impeachment.

Trial of Impeachments
Section 5.

All impeachments shall be tried by the Senate. When sitting for that purpose the Senators shall be upon oath or affirmation. No person shall be convicted without the concurrence of two-thirds of the members present.

Officers Liable to Impeachment
Section 6.

The Governor and all other civil officers shall be liable to impeachment for any misbehavior in office, but judgment in such cases shall not extend further than to removal from office and disqualification to hold any office of trust or profit under this Commonwealth. The person accused, whether convicted or acquitted, shall nevertheless be liable to indictment, trial, judgment and punishment according to law.

Removal of Civil Officers
Section 7.

All civil officers shall hold their offices on the condition that they behave themselves well while in office, and shall be removed on conviction of misbehavior in office or of any infamous crime. Appointed civil officers, other than judges of the courts of record, may be removed at the pleasure of the power by which they shall have been appointed. All civil officers elected by the people, except the Governor, the Lieutenant Governor, members of the General Assembly and judges of the courts of record, shall be removed by the Governor for reasonable cause, after due notice and full hearing, on the address of two-thirds of the Senate.

<u>Article VII</u>

ELECTIONS

Qualifications of Electors
Section 1.

Every citizen 21 years of age, possessing the following qualifications, shall be entitled to vote at all elections subject, however, to such laws requiring and regulating the registration of electors as the General Assembly may enact. 1. He or she shall have been a citizen of the United States at least one month. 2. He or she shall have resided in the State ninety (90) days immediately preceding the election. 3. He or she shall have resided in the election district where he or she shall offer to vote at least sixty (60) days immediately preceding the election, except that if qualified to vote in an election district prior to removal of residence, he or she may, if a resident of Pennsylvania, vote in the election district from which he or she removed his or her residence within sixty (60) days preceding the election.

General Election Day

Section 2.

The general election shall be held biennially on the Tuesday next following the first Monday of November in each even- numbered year, but the General Assembly may be law fix a different day, two-thirds of all the members of each House consenting thereto: Provided, that such election shall always be held in an even-numbered year.

Municipal Election Day; Offices to Be Filled on Election Days
Section 3.

All judged elected by the electors of the State at large may be elected at either a general or municipal election, as circumstances may require. All elections for judges of the courts for the several judicial districts, and for county, city, ward, borough, and township officers, for regular terms of service, shall be held on the municipal election day; namely, the Tuesday next following the first Monday of November in each odd-numbered year, but the General Assembly may by law fix a different day, two-thirds of all the members of each House consenting thereto: Provided, That such elections shall be held in an odd-numbered year: Provided further, That all judges for the courts of the several judicial districts holding office at the present time, whose terms of office may end in an odd-numbered year, shall continue to hold their offices until the first Monday of January in the next succeeding even-numbered year.

Method of Elections; Secrecy in Voting
Section 4.

All elections by the citizens shall be by ballot or by such other method as may be prescribed by law; Provided, That secrecy in voting be preserved.

Electors Privileged from Arrest
Section 5.

Electors shall in all cases except treason, felony and breach or surety of the peace, be privileged from arrest during their attendance on elections and in going to and returning therefrom.

Election and Registration Laws
Section 6.

All laws regulating the holding of elections by the citizens, or for the registration of electors, shall be uniform throughout the State, except that laws regulating and requiring the registration of electors may be enacted to apply to cities only, provided that such laws be uniform for cities of the same class, and except further, that the General Assembly shall by general law, permit the use of voting machines, or other mechanical devices for registering or recording and computing the vote, at all elections or primaries, in any county, city, borough, incorporated town or township of the Commonwealth, at the option of the electors of such county, city, borough, incorporated town or township, without being obliged to require the use of such voting machines or mechanical devices in any other county, city, borough, incorporated town or township, under such regulations with reference thereto as the General Assembly may from time to time prescribe. The General Assembly may, from time to time, prescribe the number and duties of election officers in any political subdivision of the Commonwealth in which voting machines or other mechanical devices authorized by this section may be used.

Bribery of Electors
Section 7.

Any person who shall give, or promise or offer to give, to an elector, any money, reward or other valuable consideration for his vote at an election, or for withholding the same, or who shall give or promise to give such consideration to any other person or party for such elector's vote for the withholding thereof, and any elector who shall receive or agree to receive, for himself or for another, any money, reward or other valuable consideration for his vote at an election, or for withholding the same, shall thereby forfeit the right to vote at such election, and any elector whose right to vote shall be challenged for such cause before the election officers, shall be required to swear or affirm that the matter of the challenge is untrue before his vote shall be received.

Witnesses in Contested Elections
Section 8.

In trials of contested elections and in proceedings for the investigation of elections, no person shall be permitted to withhold his testimony upon the ground that it may criminate himself or subject him to public infamy; but such testimony shall not afterwards be used against him in any judicial proceedings except for perjury in giving such testimony.

Fixing Election Districts
Section 9.

Townships and wards of cities or boroughs shall form or be divided into election districts of compact and contiguous territory and their boundaries fixed and changed in such manner as may be provided by law.

Viva Voce Elections
Section 10.

All elections by persons in a representative capacity shall be viva voce or by automatic recording device publicly indicating how each person voted.

Election Officers
Section 11.

District election boards shall consist of a judge and two inspectors, who shall be chosen at municipal elections for such terms as may be provided by law. Each elector shall have the right to vote for the judge and one inspector, and each inspector shall appoint one clerk. The first election board for any new district shall be selected, and vacancies in election boards filled, as shall be provided by law. Election officers shall be privileged from arrest upon days of election, and while engaged in making up and transmitting returns, except upon warrant of a court of record or judge thereof, for an election fraud, for felony, or for wanton breach of the peace. In cities they may claim exemption from jury during their terms of service.

Disqualifications for Service as Election Officer
Section 12.

No person shall be qualified to serve as an election officer who shall hold, or shall within two months have held any office, appointment or employment in or under the government of the United States, or of this State, or of any city, or county, or of any municipal board, commission or trust in any city, save only notaries public and persons in the National Guard or in a reserve component of the armed forces of the United States; nor shall any election officer be eligible to any civil office to be filled at an election at which he shall serve, save only to such subordinate municipal or local offices, below the grade of city or county offices, as shall be designated by general law.

Contested Elections
Section 13.

The trial and determination of contested elections of electors of President and Vice-President, members of the General Assembly, and of all public officers, whether State, judicial, municipal or local, and contests involving questions submitted to the electors at any election shall be by the courts of law, or by one or more of the law judges thereof. The General Assembly shall, by general law, designate the courts and judges by whom the several classes of election contests shall be tried and regulate the manner of trial and all matters incident thereto; but no such law assigning jurisdiction, or regulating its exercise, shall apply to any contest arising out of an election held before its passage.

Absentee Voting
Section 14.

(a) The Legislature shall, by general law, provide a manner in which, and the time and place at which, qualified electors who may, on the occurrence of any election, be absent from the municipality of their residence, because their duties, occupation or business require them to be elsewhere or who, on the occurrence of any election, are unable to attend at their proper polling places because of illness or physical disability or who will not attend a polling place because of the observance of a religious holiday or who cannot vote because of election day duties, in the case of a county employee, may vote, and for the return and canvass of their votes in the election district in which they respectively reside.

(b) For purposes of this section, "municipality" means a city, borough, incorporated town, township or any similar general purpose unit of government which may be created by the General Assembly.

<u>Article VIII</u>

TAXATION AND FINANCE

Uniformity of Taxation
Section 1.

All taxes shall be uniform, upon the same class of subjects, within the territorial limits of the authority levying the tax, and shall be levied and collected under general laws.

Exemptions and Special Provisions
Section 2.

(a) The General Assembly may by law exempt from taxation:

(i) Actual places of regularly states religious worship:

(ii) Actual places of burial, when used or held by a person or organization deriving no private or corporate profit therefrom and no substantial part of whose activity consists of selling personal property in connection therewith;

(iii) That portion of public property which is actually and regularly used for public purposes;

(iv) That portion of the property owned and occupied by any branch, post or camp of honorably discharged servicemen or servicewomen which is actually and regularly used for benevolent, charitable or patriotic purposes; and

(v) Institutions of purely public charity, but in the case of any real property tax exemptions only that portion of real property of such institution which is actually and regularly used for the purposes of the institution.

(b) The General Assembly may, by law:

(i) Establish standards and qualifications for private forest reserves, agriculture reserves, and land actively devoted to agriculture use, and make special provision for the taxation thereof;

(ii) Establish as a class or classes of subjects of taxation the property or privileges of persons who, because of age, disability, infirmity or poverty are determined to be in need of tax exemption or of special tax provisions, and for any such class or classes and standards and qualifications, and except as herein provided may impose taxes, grant exemptions, or make special tax provisions in accordance therewith. No exemption or special provision shall be made under this clause with respect to taxes upon the sale or use of personal property, and no exemption from any tax upon real property shall be granted by the General Assembly under this clause unless the General Assembly shall provide for the reimbursement of local taxing authorities by or through the Commonwealth for revenue losses occasioned by such exemption;

(iii) Establish standards and qualifications by which local taxing authorities may make uniform special tax provisions applicable to a taxpayer for a limited period of time to encourage improvement of deteriorating property or areas by an individual, association or corporation, or to encourage industrial development by a non- profit corporation; and

(iv) Make special tax provisions on any increase in value of real estate resulting from residential construction. Such special tax provisions shall be applicable for a period not to exceed two years.

(v) Establish standards and qualifications by which local taxing authorities in counties of the first and second class make uniform special real property tax provisions applicable to taxpayers who are long-time owner-occupants as shall be defined by the General Assembly of residences in areas where real property values have risen markedly as a consequence of the refurbishing or renovating of other deteriorating residences or the construction of new residences.

(vi) Authorize local taxing authorities to exclude from taxation an amount based on the assessed value of homestead property. The exclusions authorized by this clause shall not exceed one-half of the median assessed value of all homestead property within a local taxing jurisdiction. A local taxing authority may not increase the millage rate of its tax on real property to pay for these exclusions.

(c) Citizens and residents of this Commonwealth, who served in any war or armed conflict in which the United States was engaged and were honorably discharged or released under honorable circumstances from active service, shall be exempt from the payment of all real property taxes upon the residence occupied by the said citizens and residents of this Commonwealth imposed by the Commonwealth of Pennsylvania or any of its political subdivisions if, as a result of military service, they are blind, paraplegic or double or quadruple arnputees or have a service-connected disability declared by the United States Veterans Administration or its successor to be a total or 100% permanent disability, and if the State Veterans' Commission determines that such persons are in need of the tax exemptions granted herein. This exemption shall be extended to the unmarried surviving spouse upon the death of an eligible veteran provided that the State Veterans' Commission determines that such person is in need of the exemption.

Reciprocal Exemptions
Section 3.

Taxation laws may grant exemptions or rebates to residents, or estates of residents, of other States which grant similar exemptions or rebates to residents, or estates of residents, of Philadelphia.

Public Utilities
Section 4.

The real property of public utilities is subject to real estate taxes imposed by local taxing authorities. Payment to the Commonwealth of gross receipts taxes or other special taxes in replacement of gross receipts taxes by a public utility and the distribution by the Commonwealth to the local taxing authorities of the amount as herein provided shall, however, be in lieu of local taxes upon its real property which is used or useful in furnishing its public utility service. The amount raised annually by such gross receipts or other special taxes shall not be less than the gross amount of real estate taxes which the local taxing authorities could have imposed upon such real property but for the exemption herein provided. This gross amount shall be determined in the manner provided by law. An amount equivalent to such real estate taxes shall be distributed annually among all local taxing authorities in the proportion which the total tax receipts of each local taxing authority bear to the total tax receipts of all local taxing authorities, or in such other equitable proportions as may be provided by law. Notwithstanding the provisions of this section, any law which presently subjects real property of public utilities to local real estate taxation by local taxing authorities shall remain in full force and effect.

Exemption from Taxation Restricted
Section 5.

All laws exempting property from taxation, other than the property above enumerated, shall be void.

Taxation of Corporations
Section 6.

The power to tax corporations and corporate property shall not be surrendered or suspended by any contract or grant to which the Commonwealth shall be a party.

Commonwealth Indebtedness
Section 7.

(a) No debt shall be incurred by or on behalf of the Commonwealth except by law and in accordance with the provisions of this section.

(1) Debt may be incurred without limit to suppress insurrection, rehabilitate areas affected by man-made or natural disaster, or to implement unissued authority approved by the electors prior to the adoption of this article.

(2) The Governor, State Treasurer and Auditor General, acting jointly, may

(i) issue tax anticipation notes having a maturity within the fiscal year of issue and payable exclusively from revenues received in the same fiscal year, and (ii) incur debt for the purpose of refunding other debt, if such refunding debt matures within the term of the original debt.

(3) Debt may be incurred without limit for purposes specifically itemized in the law authorizing such debt, if the question whether the debt shall be incurred has been submitted to the electors and approved by a majority of those voting on the question.

(4) Debt may be incurred without the approval of the electors for capital projects specifically itemized in a capital budget, if such debt will not cause the amount of all net debt outstanding to exceed one and three-quarters times the average of the annual tax revenues deposited in the previous five fiscal years as certified by the Auditor General. For the purposes of this subsection, debt outstanding shall not include debt incurred under clauses (1) and (2) (i), or debt incurred under clause (2) (ii) if the original debt would not be so considered, or debt incurred under subsection (3) unless the General Assembly shall so provide in the law authorizing such debt.

(b) All debt incurred for capital projects shall mature within a period not to exceed the estimated useful life of the projects as stated in the authorizing law, and when so stated shall be conclusive. All debt, except indebtedness permitted by clause (2) (i), shall be amortized in substantial and regular amounts, the first of which shall be due prior to the expiration of a period equal to one-tenth the term of the debt.

(c) As used in this section, debt shall mean the issued and outstanding obligations of the Commonwealth and shall include obligations of its agencies or authorities to the extent they are to be repaid from lease rentals or other charges payable directly or indirectly from revenues of the Commonwealth. debts shall not include either (1) that portion of obligations to be repaid from charges made to the public for the use of the capital projects financed, as determined by the Auditor General, or (2) obligations to be repaid from lease rentals or other charges payable by a school district or other local taxing authority, (3) obligations to be repaid by agencies or authorities created for the joint benefit of the Commonwealth and one or more other State governments.

(d) If sufficient funds are not appropriated for the timely payment of the interest upon and installments of principal of all debt, the State Treasurer shall set apart from the first revenues thereafter received applicable to the appropriate fund a sum sufficient to pay such interest and installments of principal, and shall so apply the money so set apart. The State Treasurer may be required to set aside and apply such revenues at the suit of any holder of Commonwealth obligations.

Commonwealth Credit Not to Be Pledged
Section 8.

The credit of the Commonwealth shall not be pledged or loaned to any individual, company, corporation or association nor shall the Commonwealth become a joint owner or stockholder in any company, corporation or association.

Municipal Debt Not to be Assumed by Commonwealth

Section 9.

The Commonwealth shall not assume the debt, or any part thereof, of any county, city, borough, incorporated town, township or any similar general purpose unit of government unless such debt shall have been incurred to enable the Commonwealth to suppress insurrection or to assist the Commonwealth in the discharge of any portion of its present indebtedness.

Audit
Section 10.

The financial affairs of any entity funded or financially aided by the Commonwealth, and all departments, boards, commissions, agencies, instrumentalities, authorities and institutions of the Commonwealth, shall be subject to audits made in accordance with generally accepted auditing standards. Any Commonwealth officer whose approval is necessary for any transaction relative to the financial affairs of the Commonwealth shall not be charged with the function of auditing that transaction after its occurrence.

Gasoline Taxes and Motor License Fees Restricted
Section 11.

(a) All proceeds from gasoline and other motor fuel excise taxes, motor vehicle registration fees and license taxes, operators' license fees and other excise taxes imposed on products used in motor transportation after providing therefrom for (a) cost of administration and collection, (b) payment of obligations incurred in the construction and reconstruction of public highways and bridges shall be appropriated by the General Assembly to agencies of the State or political subdivisions thereof; and used solely for construction, reconstruction, maintenance and repair of and safety on public highways and bridges and costs and expenses incident thereto, and for the payment of obligations incurred for such purposes, and shall not be diverted by transfer or otherwise to any other purpose, except that loans may be made by the State from the proceeds of such taxes and fees for a single period not exceeding eight months, but no such loan shall be made within the period of one year from any preceding loan, and every loan made in any fiscal year shall be repayable within one month after the beginning of the next fiscal year.

(b) All proceeds from aviation fuel excise taxes, after providing therefrom for the cost of administration and collection, shall be appropriated by the General Assembly to agencies of the State or political subdivisions thereof and used solely for: the purchase, construction, reconstruction, operation and maintenance of airports and other air navigation facilities; aircraft accident investigation; the operation, maintenance and other costs of aircraft owned or leased by the Commonwealth; any other purpose reasonable related to air navigation including but not limited to the reimbursement of airport property owners for property tax expenditures; and costs and expenses incident thereto and for the payment of obligations incurred for such purposes, and shall not be diverted by transfer or otherwise to any other purpose.

Governor's Budgets and Financial Plan
Section 12.

Annually, at the times set by law, the Governor shall submit to the General Assembly:

(a) A balanced operating budget for the ensuing fiscal year setting forth in detail (i) proposed expenditures classified by department or agency and by program and (ii) estimated revenues from all sources. If estimated revenues and available surplus are less than proposed expenditures, the Governor shall recommend specific additional sources of revenue sufficient to pay the deficiency and the estimated revenue to be derived from each source;

(b) A capital budget for the ensuing fiscal year setting forth in detail proposed expenditures to be financed from the proceeds of obligations of the Commonwealth or of its agencies or authorities or from operating funds; and

(c) A financial plan for not less than the next succeeding five fiscal years, which plan shall include for each such fiscal year:

(i) Projected operating expenditures classified by department or agency and by program, in reasonable detail, and estimated revenues, by major categories, from existing and additional sources, and

(ii) Projected expenditures for capital projects specifically itemized by purpose, and the proposed sources of financing each.

Appropriations
Section 13.

(a) Operating budget appropriations made by the General Assembly shall not exceed the actual and estimated revenues and surplus available in the same fiscal year.

(b) The General Assembly shall adopt a capital budget for the ensuing fiscal year.

Surplus
Section 14.

All surplus of operating funds at the end of the fiscal year shall be appropriated during the ensuing fiscal year by the General Assembly.

Project "70"
Section 15.

In addition to the purposes stated in Article VIII, section seven of this Constitution, the Commonwealth may be authorized by law to create debt and to issue bonds to the amount of $70,000,000 for the acquisition of land for State parks, reservoirs and other conservation and recreation and historical preservation purposes, and for participation by the Commonwealth with political subdivisions in the acquisition of land for parks, reservoirs and other conservation and recreation and historical preservation purposes, subject to such conditions and limitations as the General Assembly may prescribe.

Land and Water Conservation and Reclamation Fund
Section 16.

In addition to the purposed stated in Article VIII, section seven of this Constitution, the Commonwealth may be authorized by law to create a debt and issue bonds in the amount of $500,000,000 for a Land and Water Conservation and reclamation Fund to be used for the conservation and reclamation of land and water resources of the Commonwealth, including the elimination of acid mine drainage, sewage, and other pollution from the streams of the Commonwealth, the provision of State financial assistance to political subdivisions and municipal authorities of the Commonwealth of Pennsylvania for the construction of sewage treatment plants, the restoration of abandoned strip-mined areas, the control and extinguishment of surface and underground mine fires, the alleviation and prevention of subsidence resulting from mining operations, and the acquisition of additional lands and the reclamation and development of part and recreational lands acquired pursuant to the authority of Article VII, section 15 of this Constitution, subject to such conditions and liabilities as the General Assembly may prescribe.

Special Emergency Legislation
Section 17.

(a) Notwithstanding any provisions of this Constitution to the contrary, the General Assembly shall have the authority to enact laws providing for tax rebates, credits exemptions, grants-in-aid, State supplementations, or otherwise provide special provisions for individuals, corporations, associations or nonprofit institutions, including nonpublic schools (whether sectarian or nonsectarian) in order to alleviate the danger, damage, suffering or hardship faced by such individuals, corporations, associations, institutions or nonpublic schools as a result of Great Storms or Floods of September 1971, of June 1972, or of 1974, or of 1975 or of 1976.

(b) Notwithstanding the provisions of Article III, section 29 subsequent to a Presidential declaration of an emergency or of a major disaster in any part of this Commonwealth, the General Assembly shall have the authority by a vote of two-thirds of all members elected to each House to make appropriations limited to moneys required for Federal emergency or major disaster relief. This subsection may apply retroactively to any Presidential declaration of an emergency or of a major disaster in 1976 or 1977.

Article IX

LOCAL GOVERNMENT

Local Government
Section 1.

The General Assembly shall provide by general law for local government within the Commonwealth. Such general law shall be uniform as to all classes of local government regarding procedural matters.

Home Rule
Section 2.

Municipalities shall have the right and power to frame and adopt home rule charters. Adoption, amendment or repeal of a home rule charter shall be by referendum. The General Assembly shall provide the procedure by which a home rule charter may be framed and its adoption, amendment or repeal presented to these electors. If the General Assembly does not so provide, a home rule charter or a procedure for framing and presenting a home rule charter may presented to the electors by initiative or by the governing body of the municipality. A municipality which has a home rule charter may exercise any power or perform any function not denied by this Constitution, by its home rule charter or by the General Assembly at any time.

Optional Plans

Section 3.

Municipalities shall have the right and power to adopt optional forms of government as provided by law. The General Assembly shall provide optional forms of government for all municipalities. An optional form of government shall be presented to the electors by initiative, by the governing body of the municipality, or by the General Assembly. Adoption or repeal of an optional form of government shall be by referendum.

County Government
Section 4.

County officers shall consist of commissioners, controllers, or auditors, district attorneys, public defenders, treasurers, sheriffs, registers of wills, recorders of deeds, prothonotaries, clerks of the courts, and such others as may from time to time be provided by law. County officers, except for public defenders who shall be appointed as shall be provided by law, shall be elected at the municipal elections and shall hold their offices for the term of four years, beginning on the first Monday of January next after their election, and until their successors shall be duly qualified; all vacancies shall be filled in such a manner as may be provided by law. County officers shall be paid only by salary as provided by law for services performed for the county or any other governmental unit. Fees incidental to the conduct of any county office shall be payable directly to the county or the Commonwealth, or as otherwise provided by law. Three county commissioners shall be elected in each county. In the election of these officers each qualified elector shall vote for no more than two persons, and the three persons receiving the highest number of votes shall be elected. Provisions for county government in this section shall apply to every county except a county which has adopted a home rule charter or an optional form of government. One of the optional forms of county government provided by law shall include the provisions of this section.

Intergovernmental Cooperation
Section 5.

A municipality by act of its governing body may, or upon being required by initiative and referendum in the area affected shall, cooperate or agree in the exercise of any function, power or responsibility with, or delegate or transfer any function, power or responsibility to, one or more other governmental unit including other municipalities or districts, the Federal government, any other state or its governmental units, or any newly created governmental unit.

Area Government
Section 6.

The General Assembly shall provide for the establishment and dissolution of government of areas involving two or more municipalities or parts thereof.

Area-wide Powers
Section 7.

The General Assembly may grant powers to area governments or to municipalities within a given geographical area in which there exists intergovernmental cooperation or area government and designate the classes of municipalities subject to such legislation.

Consolidation, Merger or Boundary Change

Section 8.

Uniform Legislation. -- The General Assembly shall, within two years following the adoption of this article, enact uniform legislation establishing the procedure for consolidation, merger or change of the boundaries of municipalities. Initiative. -- The electors of any municipality shall have the right, by initiative and referendum, to consolidate, merge and change boundaries by a majority vote of those voting thereon in each municipality, without the approval of any governing body. Study. -- The General Assembly shall designate an agency of the Commonwealth to study consolidation, merger and boundary changes, advise municipalities on all problems which might be connected therewith, and initiate local referendum. Legislative Power. -- Nothing herein shall prohibit or prevent the General Assembly from providing additional methods for consolidation, merger or change of boundaries.

Appropriation for Public Purposes
Section 9.

The General Assembly shall not authorize any municipality or incorporated district to become a stockholder in any company, association or corporation, or to obtain or appropriate money for, or to loan its credit to, any corporation, association, institution or individual. The General Assembly may provide standards by which municipalities or school districts may give financial assistance or lease property to public service, industrial or commercial enterprises if it shall find that such assistance or leasing is necessary to the health, safety or welfare of the Commonwealth or any municipality or school district. Existing authority of any municipality or incorporated district to obtain or appropriate money for, or to loan its credit to, any corporation, association, institution or individual, is preserved.

Local Government Debt
Section 10.

Subject only to the restrictions imposed by this section, the General Assembly shall prescribe the debt limits of all units of local government including municipalities and school districts. For such purposes, the debt limit base shall be a percentage of the total revenue, as defined by the General Assembly, of the unit of local government computed over a specific period immediately preceding the year of borrowing. The debt limit to be prescribed in every such case shall exclude all indebtedness (1) for any project to the extent that it is self-liquidating or self-supporting or which has heretofore been defined as self- liquidating or self-supporting, or (2) which has been approved by referendum held in such manner as shall be provided by law. The provisions of this paragraph shall not apply to the City or County of Philadelphia. Any unit of local government, including municipalities and school districts, incurring any indebtedness, shall at or before the time of so doing adopt a covenant, which shall be binding upon it so long as any such indebtedness shall remain unpaid, to make payments out of its sinking fund or any other of its revenues or funds at such time and in such annual amounts specified in such covenant as shall be sufficient for the payment of the interest thereon and the principal thereof when due.

Local Reapportionment
Section 11.

Within the year following that in which the Federal decennial census is officially reported as required by Federal law, and at such other times as the governing body of any municipality shall deem necessary, each municipality having a governing body not entirely elected at large shall be reapportioned, by its governing body or as shall otherwise be provided by uniform law, into districts which shall be composed of compact and contiguous territory as nearly equal in population as practicable, for the purpose of describing the districts for those not elected at large.

Philadelphia Debt
Section 12.

The debt of the City of Philadelphia may be increased in such amount that the total debt of said city shall not exceed thirteen and one-half percent of the average of the annual assessed valuations of the taxable realty therein, during the ten years immediately preceding the year in which such increase is made, but said city shall not increase its indebtedness to an amount exceeding three percent upon such average assessed valuation of realty, without the consent of the electors thereof at a public election held in such manner as shall be provided by law. In ascertaining the debt-incurring capacity of the City of Philadelphia at any time, there shall be deducted from the debt of said city so much of such debt as shall have been incurred, or is about to be incurred, and the proceeds thereof expended, or about to be expended, upon any public improvement, or in construction, purchase or condemnation of any public utility, or part thereof, or facility therefor, if such public improvement or public utility, or part thereof, or facility therefor, may reasonable be expected to yield revenue in excess of operating expenses sufficient to pay the interest and sinking fund charges thereon. The method of determining such amount, so to be deducted, shall be as now prescribed, or which may hereafter be prescribed by law. In incurring indebtedness for any purpose the City of Philadelphia may issue its obligations maturing not later than fifty years from the date thereof, with provision for a sinking fund to be in equal or graded annual or other periodical installments. Where any indebtedness shall be or shall have been incurred by said City of Philadelphia for the purpose of the construction or improvement of public works or utilities of any character, from which income or revenue is to be derived by said city, or for the reclamation of land to be used in the construction of wharves or docks owned or to be owned by said city, such obligations may be in an amount sufficient to provide for, and may include the amount of the interest and sinking fund charges accruing and which may accrue thereon throughout the period of construction, and until the expiration of one year after the completion of the work for which said indebtedness shall have been incurred. No debt shall be incurred by, or on behalf of, the County of Philadelphia.

Abolition of County Offices in Philadelphia
Section 13.

(a) In Philadelphia all county offices are hereby abolished, and the city shall henceforth perform all functions of county government within its area through officers selected in such manner as may be provided by law.

(b) Local and special laws, regulating the affairs of the City of Philadelphia and creating offices or prescribing the powers and duties of officers of the City of Philadelphia, shall be valid notwithstanding the provisions of section thirty-two of Article III of this Constitution.

(c) All laws applicable to the County of Philadelphia shall apply to the City of Philadelphia.

(d) The City of Philadelphia shall have, assume and take over all powers, property, obligations and indebtedness of the County of Philadelphia.

(e) The provisions of section two of this article shall apply with full force and effect to the functions of the county government hereafter to be performed by the city government.

(f) Upon adoption of this amendment all county officers shall become officers of the City of Philadelphia, and until the General Assembly shall otherwise provide, shall continue to perform their duties and be elected, appointed, compensated and organized in such manner as may be provided by the provisions of this Constitution and the laws of the Commonwealth in effect at the time this amendment becomes effective, but such officers serving when this amendment becomes effective shall be permitted to complete their terms.

Definitions
Section 14.

As used in this article, the following words shall have the following meanings:
"Municipality" means a county, city, borough, incorporated town, township or any similar general purpose unit of government which shall hereafter be created by the General Assembly.
"Initiative" means the filing with the applicable election officials at least ninety days prior to the next primary or general election of a petition containing a proposal for referendum signed by electors comprising five percent of the number of electors voting for the office of Governor in the last gubernatorial general election in each municipality or area affected. The applicable election official shall place the proposal on the ballot in a manner fairly representing the content of the petition for decision by referendum at said election. Initiative on a similar question shall not be submitted more than once in five years. No enabling law shall be required for initiative.
"Referendum" means approval of a question placed on the ballot, by initiative or otherwise, by a majority vote of the electors voting thereon.

<u>Article X</u>

PRIVATE CORPORATIONS

Certain Unused Charters Void
Section 1.

The charters and privileges granted prior to 1874 to private corporations which had not been organized in good faith and commenced business prior to 1874 shall be void.

Certain Charters to Be Subject to the Constitution
Section 2.

Private corporations which have accepted or accept the Constitution of this Commonwealth or the benefits of any law passed by the General Assembly after 1873 governing the affairs of corporations shall hold their charters subject to the provisions of the Constitution of this Commonwealth.

Revocation, Amendment and Repeal of Charters and Corporation Laws
Section 3.

All charters of private corporations and all present and future common or statutory law with respect to the formation or regulation of private corporations or prescribing powers, rights, duties or liabilities of private corporations or their officers, directors or shareholders may be revoked, amended or repealed.

Compensation for Property Taken by Corporations Under Right of Eminent Domain

Section 4.

Municipal and other corporations invested with the privilege of taking private property for public use shall make just compensation for property taken, injured or destroyed by the construction or enlargement of their works, highways or improvements and compensation shall be paid or secured before the taking, injury or destruction.

<u>Article XI</u>

AMENDMENTS

Proposal of Amendments by the General Assembly and Their Adoption
Section 1.

Amendments to this Constitution may be proposed in the Senate or House of Representatives; and if the same shall be agreed to by a majority of the members elected to each House, such proposed amendment or amendments shall be entered on their journals with the yeas and nays taken thereon, and the Secretary of the Commonwealth shall causes the same to be published three months before the next general election, in at least two newspapers in every county in which such newspapers shall be published; and if, in the General Assembly next afterwards chosen, such proposed amendment or amendments shall be agreed to by a majority of the members elected to each House, the Secretary of the Commonwealth shall cause the same again to be published in the manner aforesaid; and such proposed amendment or amendments shall be submitted to the qualified electors of the State in such manner, and at such time at least three months after being so agreed to by the two Houses, as the General Assembly shall prescribe; and, if such amendment or amendments shall be approved by a majority of those voting thereon, such amendment or amendments shall become a part of the Constitution; but no amendment or amendments shall be submitted oftener than once in five years. When two or more amendments shall be submitted they shall be voted upon separately.

(a) In the event a major emergency threatens or is about to threaten the Commonwealth and if the safety or welfare of the Commonwealth required prompt amendment of this Constitution, such amendments to this Constitution may be proposed in the Senate or House of Representatives at any regular or special session of the General Assembly, and if agreed to by at least two-thirds of the members elected to each House, a proposed amendment shall be entered on the journal of each House with the yeas and nays taken thereon and the official in charge of statewide elections shall promptly publish such proposed amendment in at least two newspapers in every county in which such newspapers are published. Such amendment shall then be submitted to the qualified electors of the Commonwealth in such manner, and at such time, at least one month after being agreed to by both Houses as the General assembly prescribes.

(b) If an emergency amendment is approved by a majority of the qualified electors voting thereon, it shall become part of this constitution. When two or more emergency amendments are submitted they shall be voted on separately.

Made in the USA
Columbia, SC
07 May 2018